W9-CLQ-437

The Betrayal, Death and Resurrection of Jesus Christ

A Puzzle
with Four Pieces

by Michael C. Nichols

DAYSTAR ✳ PUBLICATIONS

TABLE OF CONTENTS

ACKNOWLEDGEMENTS

To Merilyn Murphree, a good friend in the Everlasting Church of God: Your comments and your editing of the original manuscript were of great value. You taught me to be more concise in my writing and you made this book better.

To Marc Bailey, publisher of the Grassroots Press and owner of Books International, Inc.: Your openmindedness and enthusiasm were most encouraging to me. Your desire to "do things the right way" may make you more of a "religious zealot" than you think.

To Kim Marhefka, graphic artist: Your artistic talent and creativity are inspiring. Thank you for your patience in designing the jacket for this book.

To my daughters Heather, Kelli and Lani: You are the strength, joy and depth of emotion in my life. Your interest and encouragement during the seven years it took to write this book were very important. Each one of you is a special treasure to me.

To Rhonda: You were there when I realized I had been shown something new in the Bible. You listened as the ideas formed and helped as this book took shape. You typed, edited, proofed and helped design the cover. Thank you for your help and for being who you are - my wife and best friend for nearly thirty years. It says in Proverbs 18:22, "Whoso finds a wife finds a good thing, and obtains the favour of the Lord." With you I have been shown tremendous favor from God.

PERSONAL LETTER TO THE READERS

In the Spring of 1990, I was studying the following scriptures in the Bible.

<u>Matthew 26:34</u>
34.   Jesus said unto him (Peter), Verily I say unto thee, That this night, before the cock crow, thou shalt deny me thrice (three times).

<u>Mark 14:30</u>
30.   And Jesus saith unto him (Peter), Verily I say unto thee, That this day, even in this night, before the cock crow <u>twice</u>, thou shalt deny me thrice.

I noticed these scriptures were basically the same except Mark 14:30 contained the word "twice" and Matthew 26:34 did not. At first these scriptures seemed confusing or contradictory to me. But God says he inspired these scriptures to be written and he is not the author of confusion (II Timothy 3:16, I Corinthians 14:33), so I thought these scriptures were probably two different statements made by Jesus at two different times and I was being shown something in the Bible I hadn't seen before. To prove what I thought, I began a study of the gospels (Matthew, Mark, Luke and John) which lasted seven years and what I discovered truly amazed me. This book contains the things I learned.

I am not an ordained minister. I've never been to a seminary or received formal religious training. What I have learned, you can learn. If you will study the Bible with an open mind and really think about what you read, with God's help you too can be amazed when you discover truths you have never understood before.

FOREWORD

Several months ago Mike Nichols came to me with a book project in mind. Although I am not a member of any particular organized religion, God and I do have something going. We talk all the time; well, maybe I should say I talk and he listens.

Anyway, Mike had this notion that after six or seven years of careful study of the Gospels he had experienced an awakening of sorts. It seemed that his first-hand study of the Gospels communicated to him some ideas that contradicted lessons he'd been taught in Sunday School and what, when I was a kid, we called "Big Church."

Mike did more than most of us would; he started thinking for himself. Imagine that! His natural curiosity got the process rolling and his engineering training took over. You know how so many brilliant ideas are astoundingly simple? Mike thought of the idea of putting the four Gospels in side-by-side columns on the same page and adding blank white space in strategic places where the blank space would help the reader see a chronology taking place.

Look, I'm an expert in the intellectual property business (books and computer software) and I'm telling you, this idea is brilliant! Without changing a single character or punctuation mark of the four Gospels you can read Mike's book and get a complete picture of how things really happened in the final 36 hours of Jesus Christ's earthly life.

No single one of the Gospels tells the complete story; but placed side-by-side with white space lining things up properly, you can read the Gospels as if all four authors are all sitting with you in your living room telling the story together.

I urge you to buy this book, read it, think about it, and tell your friends. I am so impressed that I'm trying to convince Mike to do the same thing for the first two-thirds of the Gospels. I, for one, would love to read more of his side-by-side presentations.

Marc Bailey
Publisher, Grassroots Press
Owner, Books International, Inc.

The Betrayal, Death and Resurrection of Jesus Christ

A Puzzle with Four Pieces

Chapter 1

Introduction

Matthew 27:22-24 describes Pontius Pilate washing his hands to signify his innocence in the crucifixion of Jesus Christ. According to what you've been taught your entire life, do any of the translations in Table 1 correctly describe what Pilate said after he washed his hands?

Table 1		
Matthew 27:22-24		
King James Version	New International Version	Revised Standard Version
22. Pilate saith unto them, What shall I do then with Jesus which is called Christ? They all say unto him, Let him be crucified.	22. "What shall I do, then, with Jesus who is called Christ?" Pilate asked. They all answered, "Crucify him!"	22. Pilate said to them, "Then what shall I do with Jesus who is called Christ?" They all said, "Let him be crucified."
23. And the governor said, Why, what evil hath he done? But they cried out the more, saying, Let him be crucified.	23. "Why? What crime has he committed?" asked Pilate. But they shouted all the louder, "Crucify him!"	23. And he said, "Why, what evil has he done?" But they shouted all the more, "Let him be crucified."
24. When Pilate saw that he could prevail nothing, but that rather a tumult was made, he took water, and washed his hands before the multitude, saying, I am innocent of the blood of this just person: see ye *to it*.	24. When Pilate saw that he was getting nowhere, but that instead an uproar was starting, he took water and washed his hands in front of the crowd. "I am innocent of this man's blood," he said. "It is your responsibility!"	24. So when Pilate saw that he was gaining nothing, but rather that a riot was beginning, he took water and washed his hands before the crowd, saying, "I am innocent of this man's blood; see to it yourselves."

Did Pilate say
"I am innocent of the blood of this just person: see you *to it*", or
"I am innocent of this man's blood, it is your responsibility", or
"I am innocent of this man's blood; see to it yourselves"?

No, none of these translations correctly translates the last part of verse 24. In the King James Version of the Bible the words "to it" at the end of verse 24 are in italics. If you will read the instructions in the front of your Bible you will see what it means when words are written in italics. You will find that when words are written in italics it means the words are <u>not</u> part of the original Greek translation. The words, "*to it*," in verse 24 were added by the translators. The correct translation of the end of Matthew 27:24 is, "I am innocent of the blood of this just person, see ye?" After Pilate washed his hands, he held them up before the crowd and said, "I am innocent of the blood of this just person, see you (my clean hands)!"

Is this an earth-shaking revelation to you? Probably not. But can you see what critical thinking can do for your understanding of God's word? God gave us minds; he expects us to use them. Now are there other things we have not understood about the events associated with Jesus' last passover and crucifixion? For instance, did you know

In Gethsemane, the angel appeared to Jesus during his second prayer.
Pontius Pilate tried desperately to free Jesus Christ and not crucify him,
Jesus was scourged not once, but twice, before he was crucified and
Peter denied Jesus more than three times?

This book is a detailed study of the events associated with the betrayal, death and resurrection of Jesus Christ. It covers the period of time which began when Jesus told his disciples to prepare the passover meal and ended when the apostles left Galilee to go into the world to teach.

In this book you will discover a brand new way to study the gospel accounts of Matthew, Mark, Luke and John. You will learn many new things about the chronology of the events that occurred in the final hours of Jesus Christ's earthly life and his life after his resurrection from the dead. When you are finished you will know better than ever before that God himself, through four different men, wrote the gospels! No man, of himself, nor any group of men, of themselves, would have written the gospels the way they are written! With these thoughts in mind, let's begin our study of the gospels.

Chapter 2

How The Gospels Are Written

It has been established beyond a doubt that the four gospel accounts of Matthew, Mark, Luke and John were written at different times by different people anywhere from 30 to 70 years after the death of Jesus. Clearly the first writer (of the Gospel of Mark) was on his own; he had only oral history and the inspired thoughts from God to guide and help him write. But the other three authors had the benefit of being able to read or at least hear about the words of the original Gospel. In fact, the author of the book of John had the benefit of knowing about all three other Gospels. That's quite a head-start the others didn't have.

This book does not attempt to study the entire set of four Gospels; in fact, it doesn't even study one single Gospel from beginning to end. My goal in this book is to focus on the final 36 hours of Jesus' earthly life and the events associated with his burial and resurrection from the dead.

To fully understand the Gospels we must understand that God has recorded certain events in all four gospel accounts which, in effect, divide Matthew, Mark, Luke and John into definite periods of time. Each period of time begins with an event recorded in all four gospel accounts and ends with the next event recorded in all four gospel accounts. One of the periods of time we will study in this book is shown in Table 2-1.

Table 2-1			
Matthew 26:30,47	Mark 14:26,43	Luke 22:39,47	John 14:31; 18:3
			31. . . . <u>Arise</u>, let us <u>go</u> hence.
30. And when they had sung a hymn, they <u>went out</u> into the mount of Olives.	26. And when they had sung a hymn, they <u>went out</u> into the mount of Olives.	39. And he <u>came out</u>, and <u>went</u>, as he was wont, to the mount of Olives; and his disciples also followed him.	
47. . . . lo, <u>Judas</u>, one of the twelve, <u>came,</u> and with him a great multitude . . .	43. . . . <u>cometh Judas</u>, one of the twelve, and with him a great multitude . . .	47. . . . <u>behold</u> a multitude, and he that was called <u>Judas</u>, one of the twelve, went before them,	3. <u>Judas</u> then, having received a band of men and officers from the chief priests and Pharisees, <u>cometh</u> . . .

3

The period of time shown in Table 2-1 begins with an event recorded in all four gospel accounts - Jesus and his disciples leaving the goodman's house after the passover meal - and ends with the next event recorded in all four gospel accounts - Judas and the band of men arriving in the garden to take Jesus captive. The next period of time begins when Judas and the band of men arrive in the garden to take Jesus captive and ends when Peter cuts off the right ear of the high priest's servant (see Table 2-2).

Table 2-2			
Matthew 26:47,51	Mark 14:43,47	Luke 22:47,50	John 18:3,10
47. . . . lo, <u>Judas</u>, one of the twelve, <u>came</u>, and with him a great multitude with swords and staves, from the chief priests and elders of the people.	43. . . . <u>cometh Judas</u>, one of the twelve, and with him a great multitude with swords and staves, from the chief priests and the scribes and the elders.	47. . . . <u>behold</u> a multitude, and he that was called <u>Judas</u>, one of the twelve, went before them,	3. <u>Judas</u> then, having received a band of men and officers from the chief priests and Pharisees, <u>cometh</u> thither with lanterns and torches . . .
51. And, behold, one of them which were with Jesus stretched out his hand, and drew his sword, and <u>struck</u> a servant of the high priest's, and <u>smote off his ear</u>.	47. And one of them that stood by drew a sword, and <u>smote</u> a servant of the high priest, and <u>cut off his ear</u>.	50. And one of them <u>smote</u> the servant of the high priest, and <u>cut off his right ear</u>.	10. Then Simon Peter having a sword drew it, and <u>smote</u> the high priest's servant, and <u>cut off his right ear</u>. The servant's name was Malchus.

Other events recorded in all four gospel accounts are shown in Table 2-3 which begins below.

Table 2-3			
Matthew 26:58; 27:2	Mark 14:54; 15:1	Luke 22:54; 23:1	John 18:15,28
58. But <u>Peter followed him afar off</u> . . .	54. And <u>Peter followed him afar off</u>,	54. . . . And <u>Peter followed afar off</u>.	15. And <u>Simon Peter followed Jesus</u> (to high priest's house),
2. . . . they <u>led him away</u>, and delivered him <u>to Pontius Pilate</u> the governor.	1. . . . and <u>carried him away</u>, and delivered him <u>to Pilate</u>.	1. . . . and <u>led him unto Pilate</u>.	28. Then <u>led they Jesus</u> from Caiaphas <u>unto the hall of judgment</u>:

Table 2-3 (continued)			
Matthew 27:11,26,33, 35	Mark 15:2,15,22,24	Luke 23:3,25,33,34	John 18:33 John 19:16,17,23,24
11. . . . and the <u>governor asked</u> him, saying, <u>Art thou the King of the Jews?</u>	2. And <u>Pilate asked</u> him, <u>Art thou the King of the Jews?</u>	3. And <u>Pilate asked</u> him, saying, <u>Art thou the King of the Jews?</u>	33. . . . and <u>said</u> unto him, <u>Art thou the King of the Jews?</u>
26. . . . and when he had scourged Jesus, he <u>delivered him to be crucified</u>.	15. . . . and <u>delivered Jesus</u>, when he had scourged him, <u>to be crucified</u>.	25. . . . but he <u>delivered Jesus to their will</u>.	16. Then <u>delivered</u> he <u>him</u> therefore unto them <u>to be crucified</u>.
33. And when they <u>were come unto</u> a place called <u>Golgotha</u>, that is to say, a place of a skull,	22. And they <u>bring him unto</u> the place <u>Golgotha</u>, which is, being interpreted, The place of a skull.	33. And when they <u>were come to</u> the place, which is called <u>Calvary</u>,	17. . . . <u>went forth into</u> a place called the place of a skull, which is called in the Hebrew <u>Golgotha</u>:
35. . . . and <u>parted his garments</u>,	24. . . . they <u>parted his garments</u>,	34. . . . And they <u>parted his raiment</u>,	23. . . . took his <u>garments</u>, and <u>made four parts</u>, to every soldier a part; and also his coat: now the coat was without seam, woven from the top throughout. 24. They said therefore among themselves, Let us not rend it, but <u>cast lots</u> for it, whose it shall be:
<u>casting lots</u>:	<u>casting lots</u> upon them,	and <u>cast lots</u>.	

5

Table 2-3 (continued)			
Matthew 27:57,58,60 Matthew 28:1	Mark 15:43,46 Mark 16:2	Luke 23:50-52,53 Luke 24:1	John 19:38,41,42 John 20:1
57. . . . there came a rich man of Arimathaea, named <u>Joseph</u>,	43. <u>Joseph</u> of Arimathaea, an honourable counsellor,	50. And, behold, there was a man named <u>Joseph</u>, a counsellor; and he was a good man, and a just: 51. (The same had not consented to the counsel and deed of them;) he was of Arimathaea, a city of the Jews:	38. And after this <u>Joseph</u> of Arimathaea,
who also himself was <u>Jesus' disciple</u>:	which also <u>waited for the kingdom of God</u>,	who also himself <u>waited for the kingdom of God</u>.	being a <u>disciple of Jesus</u>,
58. He went to Pilate, and <u>begged</u> the <u>body of Jesus</u>.	came, and went in boldly unto Pilate, and <u>craved</u> the <u>body of Jesus</u>.	52. This man went unto Pilate, and <u>begged</u> the <u>body of Jesus</u>.	but secretly for fear of the Jews, besought Pilate that he might take away the <u>body of Jesus</u>:
60. And <u>laid it</u> (Jesus' body) in his own new tomb, which he had hewn out in the rock:	46. . . . and <u>laid him</u> in a sepulchre which was hewn out of a rock,	53. . . . and <u>laid it</u> in a sepulchre that was hewn in stone, wherein never man before was laid.	41. Now in the place where he was crucified there was a garden; and in the garden a new sepulchre, wherein was never man yet laid. 42. There <u>laid they Jesus</u> . . .
1. . . . as it began to dawn toward the first day of the week, <u>came Mary Magdalene and the other Mary</u> to see the sepulchre.	2. And very early in the morning the first day of the week, <u>they came</u> unto the sepulchre at the rising of the sun.	1. NOW upon the first day of the week, very early in the morning, <u>they came</u> unto the sepulchre,	1. THE first day of the week cometh <u>Mary Magdalene</u> early, when it was yet dark, unto the sepulchre,

These events are recorded in all four gospel accounts. But there are other events recorded in only three gospel accounts; some events are recorded in only two gospel accounts, while still others are recorded in only one. So, to fully understand what is written in Matthew, Mark, Luke and John, all of the events recorded in these four books have to be compared to determine the order in which each event occurred. An example should clarify this point. On the night before Jesus was crucified, Jesus and the disciples went to Gethsemane where Jesus prayed three times. Only Matthew and Mark mention either the three times Jesus prayed, or the three times he returned from prayer. See the scriptural comparison in Table 2-4.

Table 2-4	
Matthew 26:36-45	Mark 14:32-41
36. Then cometh Jesus with them unto a place called Gethsemane, and saith unto the disciples, Sit ye here, while I go and pray yonder. 37. And he took with him Peter and the two sons of Zebedee, and began to be sorrowful and very heavy. 38. Then saith he unto them, My soul is exceeding sorrowful, even unto death: tarry ye here, and watch with me.	32. And they came to a place which was named Gethsemane: and he saith to his disciples, Sit ye here, while I shall pray. 33. And he taketh with him Peter and James and John, and began to be sore amazed, and to be very heavy; 34. And saith unto them, My soul is exceeding sorrowful unto death: tarry ye here, and watch.
39. And he went a little farther, and fell on his face, and <u>prayed</u>, saying, O my Father, if it be possible, let this cup pass from me: nevertheless not as I will, but as thou wilt. 40. And he cometh unto the disciples, and findeth them asleep, and saith unto Peter, What, could ye not watch with me one hour? 41. Watch and pray, that ye enter not into temptation: the spirit indeed is willing, but the flesh is weak.	35. And he went forward a little, and fell on the ground, and <u>prayed</u> that, if it were possible, the hour might pass from him. 36. And he said, Abba, Father, all things are possible unto thee; take away this cup from me: nevertheless not what I will, but what thou wilt. 37. And he cometh, and findeth them sleeping, and saith unto Peter, Simon, sleepest thou? couldest not thou watch one hour? 38. Watch ye and pray, lest ye enter into temptation. The spirit truly is ready, but the flesh is weak.
42. He <u>went away again the **second time,**</u> and <u>prayed</u>, saying, O my Father, if this cup may not pass away from me, except I drink it, thy will be done. 43. And he came and found them asleep again: for their eyes were heavy.	39. And <u>**again** he went away</u>, and <u>prayed</u>, and spake the same words. 40. And when he returned, he found them asleep again, (for their eyes were heavy,) neither wist they what to answer him.
44. And he left them, and went away again, and <u>prayed the **third time,**</u> saying the same words. 45. Then <u>cometh he to his disciples</u>, and saith unto them, Sleep on now, and take your rest: behold, the hour is at hand, and the Son of man is betrayed into the hands of sinners.	41. And he <u>cometh the **third time,**</u> and saith unto them, Sleep on now, and take your rest: it is enough, the hour is come; behold, the Son of man is betrayed into the hands of sinners.

By placing the events in Matthew <u>side-by-side</u> with the <u>same</u> events in Mark, and comparing the scriptures, we can better understand what happened. In reading the scriptural comparison in Table 2-4, you may want to first read <u>across</u> to verify that the events placed side-by-side are the same events. You can then read from <u>top to bottom</u> to verify the order in which the events occurred and to determine how the story flows.

7

Now let's look more closely at Jesus' second prayer in Table 2-5.

Table 2-5	
Matthew 26:42-45	Mark 14:39-41
42. He <u>went away again the **second time**,</u> and <u>prayed</u>, saying, O my Father, if this cup may not pass away from me, except I drink it, thy will be done. 43. And he came and found them <u>asleep again</u>: for their eyes were heavy.	39. And **again** <u>he went away</u>, and <u>prayed</u>, and spake the same words. 40. And when he returned, he found them <u>asleep again</u>, (for their eyes were heavy,) neither wist they (or <u>neither knew they</u>) <u>what to answer him</u>.
44. And he left them, and went away again, and <u>prayed the **third time**,</u> saying the same words. 45. Then <u>cometh he to his disciples</u>, and saith unto them, Sleep on now, and take your rest: behold, the hour is at hand, and the Son of man is betrayed into the hands of sinners.	41. And he <u>cometh the **third time**,</u> and saith unto them, Sleep on now, and take your rest: it is enough, the hour is come; behold, the Son of man is betrayed into the hands of sinners.

After Jesus completed his second prayer in Gethsemane, he returned to his disciples and found them asleep again (Matthew 26:43, Mark 14:40 first part). He asked them a <u>question</u>, for which they had <u>no answer</u> (Mark 14:40 last part). What question did Jesus ask them? Table 2-5 shows this question is not recorded in Matthew or Mark. It is however recorded in Luke. Jesus prayed in Gethsemane <u>after</u> he and his disciples left the goodman's house but <u>before</u> Judas and the band of men arrived in the garden to take Jesus captive (Matthew 26:30-47, Mark 14:26-43). This same period of time in Luke begins in Luke 22:39 and ends in Luke 22:47 as shown in Table 2-6.

Table 2-6
<u>Luke 22:39-47</u> 39. And he came out (of the goodman's house), and went, as he was wont, to the mount of Olives; and his disciples also followed him. 40. And when he was at the place, he said unto them, Pray that ye enter not into temptation. 41. And he was withdrawn from them about a stone's cast, and kneeled down, and prayed, 42. Saying, Father, if thou be willing, remove this cup from me: nevertheless not my will, but thine, be done. 43. And there appeared an angel unto him from heaven, strengthening him. 44. And being in an agony he prayed more earnestly: and his sweat was as it were great drops of blood falling down to the ground. 45. And when he rose up from prayer, and was come to his disciples, he found them sleeping for sorrow, 46. And said unto them, **Why sleep ye?** rise and pray, lest ye enter into temptation. 47. And while he yet spake, behold a multitude, and he that was called Judas, one of the twelve, went before them, and drew near unto Jesus to kiss him.

The question for which the disciples had no answer is "Why sleep ye?" (Luke 22:46 above). Let's see why.

In Table 2-7, the "place" mentioned in the first part of Luke 22:40 is the same "place called or named Gethsemane" in Matthew 26:36 and Mark 14:32. Therefore, to better understand what really happened we position the first part of Luke 22:40 side-by-side with the verses in Matthew and Mark referenced above. The next event recorded in Luke is part of a statement Jesus made to his disciples after his first prayer. So the last part of Luke 22:40 is positioned as shown. Luke contains no record of Jesus' first prayer in Gethsemane. Table 2-7 on pages 9-10 shows all of the statements and events associated with Jesus' second prayer in Gethsemane including the appearance of the angel (Luke 22:43).

Table 2-7		
Matthew 26:36-42	Mark 14:32-39	Luke 22:40-42
36. Then cometh Jesus with them unto a place called Gethsemane, and saith unto the disciples, Sit ye here, while I go and pray yonder. 37. And he took with him Peter and the two sons of Zebedee, and began to be sorrowful and very heavy. 38. Then saith he unto them, My soul is exceeding sorrowful, even unto death: tarry ye here, and watch with me.	32. And they came to a place which was named Gethsemane: and he saith to his disciples, Sit ye here, while I shall pray. 33. And he taketh with him Peter and James and John, and began to be sore amazed, and to be very heavy; 34. And saith unto them, My soul is exceeding sorrowful unto death: tarry ye here, and watch.	40. And when he was at the place,
39. And he went a little farther, and fell on his face, and prayed, saying, O my Father, if it be possible, let this cup pass from me: nevertheless not as I will, but as thou wilt. 40. And he cometh unto the disciples, and findeth them asleep, and saith unto Peter, What, could ye not watch with me one hour? 41. Watch and pray, that ye enter not into temptation: the spirit indeed is willing, but the flesh is weak.	35. And he went forward a little, and fell on the ground, and prayed that, if it were possible, the hour might pass from him. 36. And he said, Abba, Father, all things are possible unto thee; take away this cup from me: nevertheless not what I will, but what thou wilt. 37. And he cometh, and findeth them sleeping, and saith unto Peter, Simon, sleepest thou? couldest not thou watch one hour? 38. Watch ye and pray, lest ye enter into temptation. The spirit truly is ready, but the flesh is weak.	he said unto them, Pray that ye enter not into temptation.
42. He went away again the second time, and prayed, saying, O my Father, if this cup may not pass away from me, except I drink it, thy will be done.	39. And again he went away, and prayed, and spake the same words.	41. And he was withdrawn from them about a stone's cast, and kneeled down, and prayed, 42. Saying, Father, if thou be willing, remove this cup from me: nevertheless not my will, but thine, be done.

Table 2-7 (continued)		
Matthew 26:43-45	Mark 14:40-41	Luke 22:43-46
		43. And there appeared an angel unto him from heaven, strengthening him. 44. And being in an agony he prayed more earnestly: and his sweat was as it were great drops of blood falling down to the ground. 45. And when he rose up from prayer,
43. And he came and found them asleep again: for their eyes were heavy.	40. And when he returned, he found them asleep again, (for their eyes were heavy,)	and was come to his disciples, he found them sleeping for sorrow,
		46. And said unto them, Why sleep ye?
	neither wist (neither knew) they what to answer him.	rise and pray, lest ye enter into temptation.
44. And he left them, and went away again, and prayed the third time, saying the same words. 45. Then cometh he to his disciples, and saith unto them, Sleep on now, and take your rest:	41. And he cometh the third time, and saith unto them, Sleep on now, and take your rest:	

Here is further proof that the prayer recorded in Luke 22:41-44 is Jesus' second prayer.

1. During his first prayer, Jesus fell face-down on the ground (Matthew 26:39, Mark 14:35-36 in Table 2-7 on page 9). During the prayer recorded in Luke 22:41-44, Jesus kneeled (Luke 22:41 in Table 2-7 on page 9). The word "fell" in Matthew 26:39 and Mark 14:35 is translated from the Greek word meaning to fall, fall down, or light on (Strong's Exhaustive Concordance of the Bible, Greek Dictionary of the New Testament, word #4098). The word "kneeled" in Luke 22:41 is translated from two Greek words meaning to place the knee in a horizontal posture, or to kneel (Strong's Concordance, Greek Dictionary, words #5087 and #1119). So, the prayer recorded in Luke 22:41-44 is not the first prayer.

2. After Jesus returned from offering the prayer in Luke 22:41-44 and found his disciples sleeping, he told them to, "rise and pray," lest they enter into temptation (Luke 22:46 last part in Table 2-7 above). After he returned from his third prayer and found his disciples sleeping, he told them to, "Sleep on now," and take their rest (Matthew 26:45 and Mark 14:41 above). So, the prayer recorded in Luke 22:41-44 is not the third prayer.

The narrative which begins at the top of page 11 is a paraphrased summary of the information shown in Table 2-7.

When Jesus and his disciples arrived in Gethsemane, Jesus told the disciples to sit while he went and prayed. He took Peter, James, and John deeper into the garden with him asking the others to wait behind. Jesus explained to the three with him that he was very sad and asked them to stay with him and help him watch. Jesus walked a short distance from them, fell face-down on the ground and asked his Father if there was any way he could avoid the awful death he was about to endure.

When Jesus returned from his first prayer, he found the disciples sleeping. He asked Peter, "Simon, are you sleeping? Couldn't you watch one hour?" He told the disciples, "Watch and pray, so that you won't be tempted. The spirit is willing, but your flesh is weak."

Jesus left again and went about a stone's throw from them. This time he just kneeled down and prayed again that his Father would save him from being crucified, but that, of course, God's will be done. An angel appeared to strengthen Jesus and he prayed so earnestly that his sweat was like great drops of blood falling to the ground.

When he returned and found the disciples sleeping again, he asked, "Why are you sleeping?" The disciples didn't know what to answer. Jesus told them, "Rise and pray, so that you won't be tempted."

After Jesus left and prayed the third time, he returned to his disciples and found them asleep again, but this time he didn't wake them up right away.

In Chapter 4 we will learn more about Jesus' third prayer from the book of John, but from the scriptural comparison in Table 2-7, we can see that the statements and events recorded in Matthew, Mark, Luke and John are interrelated, so much so that a question is recorded in Luke and the response to that question (or lack of response) is recorded in Mark!

The gospels are divided into periods of time and the events recorded in all four gospels have to be studied together and compared, then put together in the correct time sequence to fully understand what happened.

With this understanding, let's study the period of time which began when the disciples asked Jesus where he wanted the passover meal prepared and ended when Jesus and the disciples left the goodman's house.

Chapter 3

The Passover Meal

As the passover approached, the disciples asked Jesus where he would like to have the meal. Jesus told Peter and John to go into the city where they would meet a man carrying a pitcher of water. They were to follow that man to whatever house he entered and tell the owner of the house that Jesus wanted to celebrate the passover at that home with his disciples. Peter and John did as they were told and, indeed, encountered a man carrying a pitcher of water. Events unfolded just as Jesus had predicted and the homeowner showed the two disciples an "upper room" that was furnished and available for their use. The reader can verify the accuracy of the preceding narrative using the scriptural comparison in Table 3 pages 12-13. The preparation of the passover meal and the events that occurred during the meal are described only in Matthew, Mark and Luke, not John.

Table 3			
Matthew 26:17-18	Mark 14:12-13	Luke 22:7-10	John
17. Now the first day of the feast of unleavened bread the disciples came to Jesus, saying unto him, Where wilt thou that we prepare for thee to eat the passover?	12. And the first day of unleavened bread, when they killed the passover, his disciples said unto him, Where wilt thou that we go and prepare that thou mayest eat the passover?	7. Then came the day of unleavened bread, when the passover must be killed.	
	13. And he sendeth forth two of his disciples,	8. And he sent Peter and John, saying, Go and prepare us the passover, that we may eat.	
		9. And they said unto him, Where wilt thou that we prepare?	
18. And he said, Go into the city	and saith unto them, Go ye into the city,	10. And he said unto them, Behold, when ye are entered into the city,	

Table 3 (continued)			
Matthew 26:18-20	Mark 14:13-17	Luke 22:10-16	John
to such a man,	and there shall meet you a man bearing a pitcher of water: follow him. 14. And wheresoever he shall go in,	there shall a man meet you, bearing a pitcher of water; follow him into the house where he entereth in.	
and say unto him, The Master saith, My time is at hand; I will keep the passover at thy house with my disciples.	say ye to the goodman of the house, The Master saith, Where is the guestchamber, where I shall eat the passover with my disciples? 15. And he will shew you a large upper room furnished and prepared: there make ready for us.	11. And ye shall say unto the goodman of the house, The Master saith unto thee, Where is the guestchamber, where I shall eat the passover with my disciples? 12. And he shall shew you a large upper room furnished: there make ready.	
19. And the disciples did as Jesus had appointed them; and they made ready the passover.	16. And his disciples went forth, and came into the city, and found as he had said unto them: and they made ready the passover.	13. And they went, and found as he had said unto them: and they made ready the passover.	
20. Now when the even was come, he sat down with the twelve.	17. And in the evening he cometh with the twelve.	14. And when the hour was come, he sat down, and the twelve apostles with him. 15. And he said unto them, With desire I have desired to eat this passover with you before I suffer: 16. For I say unto you, I will not anymore eat thereof, until it be fulfilled in the kingdom of God.	**NOTES:** 1) Notes in the tables are shaded to distinguish them from the scriptures. 2) After saying how much he wanted to eat this passover with the disciples, Jesus said he would not eat it again until it was fulfilled in the kingdom of God (Luke 22:15-16).

	Table 3 (continued)		
Matthew 26:21-26	Mark 14:18-22	Luke 22:17-19	John
		17. And he took the cup, and gave thanks, and said, Take this, and divide it among yourselves: 18. For I say unto you, I will not drink of the fruit of the vine until the kingdom of God shall come.	
21. And as they did eat, he said, Verily I say unto you, that one of you shall betray me. 22. And they were exceeding sorrowful, and began every one of them to say unto him, Lord, is it I? 23. And he answered and said, He that dippeth his hand with me in the dish, the same shall betray me. 24. The Son of man goeth as it is written of him: but woe unto that man by whom the Son of man is betrayed! it had been good for that man if he had not been born. 25. Then Judas, which betrayed him, answered and said, Master, is it I? He said unto him, Thou hast said.	18. And as they sat and did eat, Jesus said, Verily I say unto you, One of you which eateth with me shall betray me. 19. And they began to be sorrowful, and to say unto him one by one, Is it I? and another said, Is it I? 20. And he answered and said unto them, It is one of the twelve, that dippeth with me in the dish. 21. The Son of man indeed goeth, as it is written of him: but woe to that man by whom the Son of man is betrayed! good were it for that man if he had never been born.		<u>NOTES</u>: 1) After giving the disciples a container of wine to be divided among themselves, Jesus said he wouldn't drink wine until the kingdom of God came (Luke 22:17-18). 2) During the discussion of Jesus' betrayal in Matthew 26:21-25 and Mark 14:18-21, the disciples, <u>one by one</u>, asked Jesus, "Lord, am I the one? . . . Is it me? . . . You can't mean me." Jesus didn't specifically identify the betrayer, but said only that it was one of the disciples. When Judas Iscariot said, "Master, you surely don't mean me," Jesus said, "That's what you say."
26. And as they were eating, Jesus took bread, and blessed it, and brake it, and gave it to the disciples, and said, Take, eat; this is my body.	22. And as they did eat, Jesus took bread, and blessed, and brake it, and gave to them, and said, Take, eat: this is my body.	19. And he took bread, and gave thanks, and brake it, and gave unto them, saying, This is my body which is given for you:	

14

Table 3 (continued)			
Matthew 26:27-29	Mark 14:23-25	Luke 22:19-20	John 13:2-5
		this do in remembrance of me.	
27. And he took the cup, and gave thanks, and gave it to them, saying, Drink ye all of it;	23. And he took the cup, and when he had given thanks, he gave it to them: and they all drank of it.	20. Likewise also the cup after supper,	
28. For this is my blood of the new testament, which is shed for many for the remission of sins. 29. But I say unto you, I will not drink henceforth of this fruit of the vine, until that day when I drink it new with you in my Father's kingdom.	24. And he said unto them, This is my blood of the new testament, which is shed for many. 25. Verily I say unto you, I will drink no more of the fruit of the vine, until that day that I drink it new in the kingdom of God.	saying, This cup is the new testament in my blood, which is shed for you.	

NOTES:

1) Jesus' statement in Matthew 26:29 and Mark 14:25 above and his statement in Luke 22:18 on page 14 are similar in content, but they were stated at different times. The statement in Luke 22:18 was made before Jesus gave the disciples the symbolic bread and wine (Luke 22:19-20). His statement in Matthew 26:29 and Mark 14:25 was made after he gave them the bread and wine (Matthew 26:26-28, Mark 14:22-24). Apparently, the wine Jesus gave the disciples in Luke 22:18 was the wine to be drunk with the meal.

2) Matthew 26:21-28 and Mark 14:18-24 show that Jesus discussed his betrayal with his disciples before he gave them the bread and wine. Luke 22:19-21 below shows that he also discussed his betrayal after the bread and wine were given.

Luke 22:19-21
  19. And he took bread, and gave thanks, and brake it, and gave unto them, saying, This is my body which is given for you: this do in remembrance of me.
  20. Likewise also the cup after supper, saying, This cup is the new testament in my blood, which is shed for you.
  21. But, behold, the hand of him that betrayeth me is with me on the table.

This second discussion of Jesus' betrayal is also described in John 13:21 on page 17 and occurred after Jesus washed the disciples' feet (John 13:2-17).

2. And supper being ended, the devil having now put into the heart of Judas Iscariot, Simon's son, to betray him;
3. Jesus knowing that the Father had given all things into his hands, and that he was come from God, and went to God;
4. He riseth from supper, and laid aside his garments; and took a towel, and girded himself.
5. After that he poureth water into a basin, and began to wash the disciples' feet, and to wipe them with the towel wherewith he was girded.

Matthew 26	Mark 14	Luke 22	John 13:6-14
			6. Then cometh he to Simon Peter: and Peter saith unto him, Lord, dost thou wash my feet?
			7. Jesus answered and said unto him, What I do thou knowest not now; but thou shalt know hereafter.
			8. Peter saith unto him, Thou shalt never wash my feet. Jesus answered him, If I wash thee not, thou hast no part with me.
			9. Simon Peter saith unto him, Lord, not my feet only, but also my hands and my head.
			10. Jesus saith to him, He that is washed needeth not save to wash his feet, but is clean every whit: and ye are clean, but not all.
			11. For he knew who should betray him; therefore said he, Ye are not all clean.
			12. So after he had washed their feet, and had taken his garments, and was set down again, he said unto them, Know ye what I have done to you?
			13. Ye call me Master and Lord: and ye say well; for so I am.
			14. If I then, your Lord and Master, have washed your feet; ye also ought to wash one another's feet.

Table 3 (continued)

| Table 3 (continued) | | | |

Matthew 26	Mark 14	Luke 22:21	John 13:15-21
			15. For I have given you an example, that ye should do as I have done to you.
			16. Verily, verily, I say unto you, The servant is not greater than his lord; neither he that is sent greater than he that sent him.
			17. If ye know these things, happy are ye if ye do them.
			18. I speak not of you all: I know whom I have chosen: but that the scripture may be fulfilled, He that eateth bread with me hath lifted up his heel against me.
			19. Now I tell you before it come, that, when it is come to pass, ye may believe that I am he.
			20. Verily, verily, I say unto you, He that receiveth whomsoever I send receiveth me; and he that receiveth me receiveth him that sent me.
			21. When Jesus had thus said, he was troubled in spirit, and testified, and said,
		21. But, behold, the hand of him that betrayeth me is with me on the table.	
			Verily, verily, I say unto you, that one of you shall betray me.

Table 3 (continued)			
Matthew 26	Mark 14	Luke 22:22-23	John 13:22-29
		22. And truly the Son of man goeth, as it was determined: but woe unto that man by whom he is <u>betrayed</u>!	
NOTES: 1) In the first discussion of Jesus' betrayal each disciple, one by one, <u>asked Jesus</u> if he was the betrayer (Matthew 26:21-25 and Mark 14:18-21 on page 14). 2) In the second discussion, the disciples inquired among themselves, or <u>asked each other</u>, who would betray Jesus (John 13:22, Luke 22:23).		23. And they began to <u>inquire among themselves</u>, which of them it was that should do this thing.	22. Then the disciples <u>looked one on another</u>, doubting of whom he spake.
			23. Now there was leaning on Jesus' bosom one of his disciples, whom Jesus loved. 24. Simon Peter therefore beckoned to him, that he should ask who it should be of whom he spake. 25. He then lying on Jesus' breast saith unto him, Lord, who is it? 26. Jesus answered, He it is, to whom I shall give a sop, when I have dipped it. And when he had dipped the sop, he gave it to Judas Iscariot, the son of Simon. 27. And after the sop Satan entered into him. Then said Jesus unto him, That thou doest, do quickly. 28. Now no man at the table knew for what intent he spake this unto him. 29. For some of them thought, because Judas had the bag,

Table 3 (continued)			
Matthew 26	Mark 14	Luke 22:24-27	John 13:29-32
			that Jesus had said unto him, Buy those things that we have need of against the feast; or, that he should give something to the poor.
30. He then having received the sop went immediately out: and it was night.
31. Therefore, when he was gone out, Jesus said, Now is the Son of man <u>glorified</u>, and God is glorified in him.
32. If God be glorified in him, God shall also <u>glorify</u> him in himself, and shall straightway glorify him.
<u>NOTE</u>: After Jesus spoke of being <u>glorified</u> (John 13:31-32), the disciples argued over who would be the <u>greatest</u> (Luke 22:24).		24. And there was also a strife among them, which of them should be accounted the <u>greatest</u>.

25. And he said unto them, The kings of the Gentiles exercise lordship over them; and they that exercise authority upon them are called benefactors.
26. But ye shall not be so: but he that is greatest among you, let him be as the younger; and he that is chief, as he that doth serve.
27. For whether is greater, he that sitteth at meat, or he that serveth? is not he that sitteth at meat? but I am | |

	Table 3 (continued)		
Matthew 26	Mark 14	Luke 22:27-32	John 13:33-35
		among you as he that serveth. 28. Ye are they which have continued with me in my temptations. 29. And I appoint unto you a kingdom, as my Father hath appointed unto me; 30. That ye may eat and drink at my table in my kingdom, and sit on thrones judging the twelve tribes of Israel.	
		31. And the Lord said, Simon, Simon, behold, Satan hath desired to have you, that he may sift you as wheat: 32. But I have prayed for thee, that thy faith fail not: and when thou art converted, strengthen thy brethren.	
NOTE: In John 13:33 Jesus told the disciples he was going somewhere they could not come. When Peter responded he was ready to follow Jesus to death (Luke 22:33 on page 21), Jesus prophesied or predicted that before the rooster crowed, Peter would deny him, or say he didn't know him, three times (John 13:38, Luke 22:34 on page 21).			33. Little children, yet a little while I am with you. Ye shall seek me: and as I said unto the Jews, Whither I go, ye cannot come; so now I say to you. 34. A new commandment I give unto you, That ye love one another; as I have loved you, that ye also love one another. 35. By this shall all men know that ye are my disciples, if ye have love one to another.

		Table 3 (continued)	
Matthew 26	Mark 14	Luke 22:33-34	John 13:36-38; 14:1-4
			36. Simon Peter said unto him, Lord, <u>whither goest thou</u>? Jesus answered him, Whither I go, thou canst not follow me now; but thou shalt follow me afterwards.
			37. Peter said unto him, Lord, why cannot I follow thee now?
		33. And he said unto him, Lord, <u>I am ready to go with thee</u>, both into prison, and <u>to death</u>.	
			<u>I will lay down my life for thy sake</u>.
			38. Jesus answered him, Wilt thou lay down thy life for my sake?
		34. And he said, I tell thee, Peter, the cock shall not crow this day, before that <u>thou shalt thrice deny that thou knowest me</u>.	Verily, verily, I say unto thee, The cock shall not crow, <u>till thou hast denied me thrice</u>.
NOTE: <u>After</u> Jesus prophesied that Peter would deny him (John 13:38 last part and Luke 22:34), but <u>before</u> Jesus and the disciples left the goodman's house (Matthew 26:30, Mark 14:26, Luke 22:39, John 14:31 last part on page 26), the conversation in John 14:1-31 and Luke 22:35-38 occurred.			1. LET not your heart be troubled: ye believe in God, believe also in me.
			2. In my Father's house are many mansions: if it were not so, I would have told you. I go to prepare a place for you.
			3. And if I go and prepare a place for you, I will come again, and receive you unto myself; that where I am, there ye may be also.
			4. And whither I go ye know, and the way ye know.

Table 3 (continued)			
Matthew 26	Mark 14	Luke 22	John 14:5-12
			5. Thomas saith unto him, Lord, we know not whither thou goest; and how can we know the way?
			6. Jesus saith unto him, I am the way, the truth, and the life: no man cometh unto the Father, but by me.
			7. If ye had known me, ye should have known my Father also: and from henceforth ye know him, and have seen him.
			8. Philip saith unto him, Lord, shew us the Father, and it sufficeth us.
			9. Jesus saith unto him, Have I been so long time with you, and yet hast thou not known me, Philip? he that hath seen me hath seen the Father; and how sayest thou then, Shew us the Father?
			10. Believest thou not that I am in the Father, and the Father in me? the words that I speak unto you I speak not of myself: but the Father that dwelleth in me, he doeth the works.
			11. Believe me that I am in the Father, and the Father in me; or else believe me for the very works' sake.
			12. Verily, verily, I say unto you, He that believeth on me,

Table 3 (continued)			
Matthew 26	Mark 14	Luke 22	John 14:12-21
			the works that I do shall he do also; and greater works than these shall he do; because I go unto my Father.
			13. And whatsoever ye shall ask in my name, that will I do, that the Father may be glorified in the Son.
			14. If ye shall ask any thing in my name, I will do it.
			15. If ye love me, keep my commandments.
			16. And I will pray the Father, and he shall give you another Comforter, that he may abide with you for ever;
			17. Even the Spirit of truth; whom the world cannot receive, because it seeth him not, neither knoweth him: but ye know him; for he dwelleth with you, and shall be in you.
			18. I will not leave you comfortless: I will come to you.
			19. Yet a little while, and the world seeth me no more; but ye see me: because I live, ye shall live also.
			20. At that day ye shall know that I am in my Father, and ye in me, and I in you.
			21. He that hath my commandments, and keepeth them, he it is that loveth me: and he that loveth me shall be

			Table 3 (continued)		
Matthew 26	Mark 14	Luke 22	John 14:21-28
			loved of my Father, and I will love him, and will manifest myself to him.
22. Judas saith unto him, not Iscariot, Lord, how is it that thou wilt manifest thyself unto us, and not unto the world?
23. Jesus answered and said unto him, If a man love me, he will keep my words: and my Father will love him, and we will come unto him, and make our abode with him.
24. He that loveth me not keepeth not my sayings: and the word which ye hear is not mine, but the Father's which sent me.
25. These things have I spoken unto you, being yet present with you.
26. But the Comforter, which is the Holy Ghost, whom the Father will send in my name, he shall teach you all things, and bring all things to your remembrance, whatsoever I have said unto you.
27. Peace I leave with you, my peace I give unto you: not as the world giveth, give I unto you. Let not your heart be troubled, neither let it be afraid.
28. Ye have heard how I said unto you, I go away, and come

	Table 3 (continued)		
Matthew 26	Mark 14	Luke 22:35-38	John 14:28-31
			again unto you. If ye loved me, ye would rejoice, because I said, I go unto the Father: for my Father is greater than I. 29. And now I have told you before it come to pass, that, when it is come to pass, ye might believe.
		35. And he said unto them, When I sent you without purse, and scrip, and shoes, lacked ye any thing? And they said, Nothing. 36. Then said he unto them, But now, he that hath a purse, let him take it, and likewise his scrip: and he that hath no sword, let him sell his garment, and buy one. 37. For I say unto you, that this that is written must yet be accomplished in me, And he was reckoned among the transgressors: for the things concerning me have an end. 38. And they said, Lord, behold, here are two swords. And he said unto them, It is enough.	
			30. Hereafter I will not talk much with you: for the prince of this world cometh, and hath nothing in me. 31. But that the world may know that I

Table 3 (continued)			
Matthew 26:30	Mark 14:26	Luke 22:39	John 14:31
			love the Father; and as the Father gave me commandment, even so I do.
30. And when they had sung an hymn, <u>they went out</u> into the mount of Olives.	26. And when they had sung an hymn, <u>they went out</u> into the mount of Olives.	39. And <u>he came out</u>, and <u>went</u>, as he was wont, to the mount of Olives; and his disciples also followed him.	Arise, let us go hence.
Jesus and the disciples leave the goodman's house.			

Chapter 4

Gethsemane

After leaving the goodman's house, Jesus talked with his disciples as they walked toward Gethsemane. This conversation is recorded in John 15:1-27 and John 16:1-32 in Table 4.

Table 4			
Matthew 26	Mark 14	Luke 22	John 15:1-6
Jesus and the disciples leave the goodman's house.			
			1. I AM the true vine, and my Father is the husbandman.
NOTE: In John 14:30 on page 25 Jesus said he wouldn't be talking with the disciples much anymore because Satan was coming. After he said this, Jesus made the statements recorded in John 15 and 16 on pages 27-34. When you first look at all of these statements, it appears he did say quite a bit, but if you look more closely and think about it, he really didn't talk much with them. The information in these two chapters can be read in about ten minutes. I would think it took longer than that to walk from the house to the mount of Olives. Also, the statements in John 15 and 16 don't appear to be a continuous conversation, but separate comments Jesus made as they walked and important thoughts came to his mind. I believe that most of the time he was walking, Jesus was in deep thought about the horrible reality of his own crucifixion and the decision he had to make - would he willingly lay down his life, or would he ask his Father to save him?			2. Every branch in me that beareth not fruit he taketh away: and every branch that beareth fruit, he purgeth it, that it may bring forth more fruit.
			3. Now ye are clean through the word which I have spoken unto you.
			4. Abide in me, and I in you. As the branch cannot bear fruit of itself, except it abide in the vine; no more can ye, except ye abide in me.
			5. I am the vine, ye are the branches: He that abideth in me, and I in him, the same bringeth forth much fruit: for without me ye can do nothing.
			6. If a man abide not in me, he is cast forth as a branch,

Table 4 (continued)			
Matthew 26	Mark 14	Luke 22	John 15:6-15
			and is withered; and men gather them, and cast them into the fire, and they are burned.
			7. If ye abide in me, and my words abide in you, ye shall ask what ye will, and it shall be done unto you.
			8. Herein is my Father glorified, that ye bear much fruit; so shall ye be my disciples.
			9. As the Father hath loved me, so have I loved you: continue ye in my love.
			10. If ye keep my commandments, ye shall abide in my love; even as I have kept my Father's commandments, and abide in his love.
			11. These things have I spoken unto you, that my joy might remain in you, and that your joy might be full.
			12. This is my commandment, That ye love one another, as I have loved you.
			13. Greater love hath no man than this, that a man lay down his life for his friends.
			14. Ye are my friends, if ye do whatsoever I command you.
			15. Henceforth I call you not servants;

			Table 4 (continued)	

Matthew 26	Mark 14	Luke 22	John 15:15-21
			for the servant knoweth not what his lord doeth: but I have called you friends; for all things that I have heard of my Father I have made known unto you.
			16. Ye have not chosen me, but I have chosen you, and ordained you, that ye should go and bring forth fruit, and that your fruit should remain: that whatsoever ye shall ask of the Father in my name, he may give it you.
			17. These things I command you, that ye love one another.
			18. If the world hate you, ye know that it hated me before it hated you.
			19. If ye were of the world, the world would love his own: but because ye are not of the world, but I have chosen you out of the world, therefore the world hateth you.
			20. Remember the word that I said unto you, The servant is not greater than his lord. If they have persecuted me, they will also persecute you; if they have kept my saying, they will keep yours also.
			21. But all these things will they do unto

Table 4 (continued)			
Matthew 26	Mark 14	Luke 22	John 15:21-27; 16:1-2
			you for my name's sake, because they know not him that sent me.
			22. If I had not come and spoken unto them, they had not had sin: but now they have no cloak for their sin.
			23. He that hateth me hateth my Father also.
			24. If I had not done among them the works which none other man did, they had not had sin: but now have they both seen and hated both me and my Father.
			25. But this cometh to pass, that the word might be fulfilled that is written in their law, They hated me without a cause.
			26. But when the Comforter is come, whom I will send unto you from the Father, even the Spirit of truth, which proceedeth from the Father, he shall testify of me:
			27. And ye also shall bear witness, because ye have been with me from the beginning.
			1. THESE things have I spoken unto you, that ye should not be offended.
			2. They shall put you out of the synagogues: yea, the time cometh,

Table 4 (continued)			
Matthew 26	Mark 14	Luke 22	John 16:2-10
			that whosoever killeth you will think that he doeth God service.
			3. And these things will they do unto you, because they have not known the Father, nor me.
			4. But these things have I told you, that when the time shall come, ye may remember that I told you of them. And these things I said not unto you at the beginning, because I was with you.
			5. But now I go my way to him that sent me; and none of you asketh me, Whither goest thou?
			6. But because I have said these things unto you, sorrow hath filled your heart.
			7. Nevertheless I tell you the truth; It is expedient for you that I go away: for if I go not away, the Comforter will not come unto you; but if I depart, I will send him unto you.
			8. And when he is come, he will reprove the world of sin, and of righteousness, and of judgment:
			9. Of sin, because they believe not on me;
			10. Of righteousness, because I go to my Father, and ye see

Table 4 (continued)			
Matthew 26	Mark 14	Luke 22	John 16:10-18
			me no more;
			11. Of judgment, because the prince of this world is judged.
			12. I have yet many things to say unto you, but ye cannot bear them now.
			13. Howbeit when he, the Spirit of truth, is come, he will guide you into all truth: for he shall not speak of himself; but whatsoever he shall hear, that shall he speak: and he will shew you things to come.
			14. He shall glorify me: for he shall receive of mine, and shall shew it unto you.
			15. All things that the Father hath are mine: therefore said I, that he shall take of mine, and shall shew it unto you.
			16. A little while, and ye shall not see me: and again, a little while, and ye shall see me, because I go to the Father.
			17. Then said some of his disciples among themselves, What is this that he saith unto us, A little while, and ye shall not see me: and again, a little while, and ye shall see me: and, Because I go to the Father?
			18. They said therefore, What is this that he saith, A

Table 4 (continued)

Matthew 26	Mark 14	Luke 22	John 16:18-23
			little while? we cannot tell what he saith.
			19. Now Jesus knew that they were desirous to ask him, and said unto them, Do ye inquire among yourselves of that I said, A little while, and ye shall not see me: and again, a little while, and ye shall see me?
			20. Verily, verily, I say unto you, That ye shall weep and lament, but the world shall rejoice: and ye shall be sorrowful, but your sorrow shall be turned into joy.
			21. A woman when she is in travail hath sorrow, because her hour is come: but as soon as she is delivered of the child, she remembereth no more the anguish, for joy that a man is born into the world.
			22. And ye now therefore have sorrow: but I will see you again, and your heart shall rejoice, and your joy no man taketh from you.
			23. And in that day ye shall ask me nothing. Verily, verily, I say unto you, Whatsoever ye shall ask the Father in my name, he will give it you.

Table 4 (continued)

Matthew 26	Mark 14	Luke 22	John 16:24-31
			24. Hitherto have ye asked nothing in my name: ask, and ye shall receive, that your joy may be full.
			25. These things have I spoken unto you in proverbs: but the time cometh, when I shall no more speak unto you in proverbs, but I shall shew you plainly of the Father.
			26. At that day ye shall ask in my name: and I say not unto you, that I will pray the Father for you:
			27. For the Father himself loveth you, because ye have loved me, and have believed that I came out from God.
			28. I came forth from the Father, and am come into the world: again, I leave the world, and go to the Father.
			29. His disciples said unto him, Lo, now speakest thou plainly, and speakest no proverb.
			30. Now are we sure that thou knowest all things, and needest not that any man should ask thee: by this we believe that thou camest forth from God.
			31. Jesus answered them, Do ye now believe?

			Table 4 (continued)
Matthew 26:31-34	Mark 14:27-30	Luke 22	John 16:32
			32. Behold, the hour cometh, yea, is now come, that ye shall be <u>scattered</u>, every man to his own, and shall leave me alone: and yet I am not alone, because the Father is with me.

Matthew 26:31-34	Mark 14:27-30	NOTES (Luke 22 / John 16:32)

31. Then saith Jesus unto them, All ye shall be <u>offended</u> because of me this night: for it is written, I will smite the shepherd, and the sheep of the flock shall be <u>scattered</u> abroad.
32. But after I am risen again, I will go before you into Galilee.
 	
33. Peter answered and said unto him, Though all men shall be offended because of thee, yet will I <u>never be offended</u>.
34. Jesus said unto him, Verily I say unto thee, That <u>this night, before the cock crow, thou shalt deny me thrice</u>.
	27. And Jesus saith unto them, All ye shall be <u>offended</u> because of me this night: for it is written, I will smite the shepherd, and the sheep shall be <u>scattered</u>.
	
	28. But after that I am risen, I will go before you into Galilee.
	
	29. But Peter said unto him, Although all shall be offended, yet will not I.
	30. And Jesus saith unto him, Verily I say unto thee, That this day, even in this night, <u>before the cock crow **twice**, thou shalt deny me thrice</u>.
		<u>NOTES</u>:
		1) The <u>scattering</u> of the disciples is described in John 16:32, Matthew 26:31 and Mark 14:27.
		2) The word "again" in Matthew 26:32 is more correctly translated "up" (Strong's Concordance, Greek Dictionary, word #1453).
		3) After Jesus said that all the disciples would be offended or frightened because of what was going to happen to him (Matthew 26:31, Mark 14:27), Peter said he <u>wouldn't be frightened</u> (Matthew 26:33). Jesus told Peter that he would be so frightened that night that he would deny him three times before the rooster crowed (Matthew 26:34). This statement in Matthew 26:34:
		  * Occurred <u>after</u> Jesus and the disciples left the goodman's house (Matthew 26:30 on page 26) and
		  * Is the <u>second</u> time Jesus told Peter that before the rooster crowed he would deny him three times. The first time occurred earlier in the evening <u>before</u> Jesus and the disciples left the goodman's house (Luke 22:34 and John 13:38 last part on page 21).
		4) After Jesus told Peter that he would deny him three times before the rooster crowed (Matthew 26:34), Peter argued with him (Mark 14:29). Jesus then told Peter that during that day, even in that night, before the rooster crowed **TWICE**, he would say he didn't know him three times (Mark 14:30). Jesus' statements in Matthew 26:34 and Mark 14:30 will be discussed in greater detail in Chapter 6 and you will clearly see that these statements occurred in the order described.
		5) Just before they arrived at Gethsemane, where Jesus became <u>very sorrowful</u> (Matthew 26:36-37, Mark 14:32-33 and Luke 22:40 first part on page 36), Jesus offered the disciples the <u>encouragement</u> in John 16:33 on page 36.

Table 4 (continued)			
Matthew 26:35-39	Mark 14:31-36	Luke 22:40	John 16:33
35. Peter said unto him, Though I should die with thee, yet will I not deny thee. Likewise also said all the disciples.	31. But he spake the more vehemently, If I should die with thee, I will not deny thee in any wise. Likewise also said they all.		
			33. These things I have spoken unto you, that in me ye might have peace. In the world ye shall have tribulation: but be of good cheer; I have overcome the world.
36. Then cometh Jesus with them unto a place called Gethsemane, and saith unto the disciples, Sit ye here, while I go and pray yonder.	32. And they came to a place which was named Gethsemane: and he saith to his disciples, Sit ye here, while I shall pray.	40. And when he was at the place,	
37. And he took with him Peter and the two sons of Zebedee, and began to be sorrowful and very heavy.	33. And he taketh with him Peter and James and John, and began to be sore amazed, and to be very heavy;		
38. Then saith he unto them, My soul is exceeding sorrowful, even unto death: tarry ye here, and watch with me.	34. And saith unto them, My soul is exceeding sorrowful unto death: tarry ye here, and watch.		
39. And he went a little farther, and fell on his face, and prayed,	35. And he went forward a little, and fell on the ground, and prayed that, if it were possible, the hour might pass from him.		
saying, O my Father,	36. And he said, Abba, Father, all things are possible unto thee;		

36

Table 4 (continued)

Matthew 26:39-43	Mark 14:36-40	Luke 22:40-45	John 16
if it be possible, let this cup pass from me: nevertheless not as I will, but as thou wilt. 40. And he cometh unto the disciples, and findeth them <u>asleep</u>, and saith unto Peter, What, could ye not watch with me one hour? 41. <u>Watch and pray</u>, that ye enter not into temptation: the spirit indeed is willing, but the flesh is weak.	take away this cup from me: nevertheless not what I will, but what thou wilt. 37. And he cometh, and findeth them <u>sleeping</u>, and saith unto Peter, Simon, sleepest thou? couldest not thou watch one hour? 38. <u>Watch ye and pray</u>, lest ye enter into temptation. The spirit truly is ready, but the flesh is weak.	he said unto them, <u>Pray</u> that ye enter not into temptation.	
42. He went away <u>again</u> the <u>second time</u>, and prayed, saying, O my Father, if this cup may not pass away from me, except I drink it, thy will be done. 43. And he came and found them <u>asleep again</u>: for their eyes were heavy.	39. And <u>again</u> he went away, and prayed, and spake the same words. 40. And when he returned, he found them <u>asleep again</u>, (for their eyes were heavy,)	41. And he was withdrawn from them about a stone's cast, and kneeled down, and prayed, 42. Saying, Father, if thou be willing, remove this cup from me: nevertheless not my will, but thine, be done. 43. And there appeared an angel unto him from heaven, strengthening him. 44. And being in an agony he <u>prayed</u> more earnestly: and his sweat was as it were great drops of blood falling down to the ground. 45. And when he rose up from prayer, and was come to his disciples, he found them <u>sleeping</u> for sorrow,	

Table 4 (continued)			
Matthew 26:44	Mark 14:40	Luke 22:46	John 17:1-5
	neither wist they what to answer him.	46. And said unto them, <u>Why sleep ye</u>? <u>rise and pray</u>, lest ye enter into temptation.	
44. And he left them, and went away again, and <u>prayed</u> the <u>third time</u>, saying the same words. **NOTE:** Jesus' <u>third prayer</u> in Gethsemane is the prayer described in Matthew 26:44 and John 17:1-26. In this prayer, Jesus asked again that his Father save him from being crucified (Matthew 26:44). Between the time he asked his Father to save him and the time he offered the prayer recorded in John 17:1-26, Jesus decided to sacrifice his life for the sins of all mankind. It was Jesus' decision (John 10:17-18). If Jesus had asked, his Father would have sent more than twelve legions of angels to save him (Matthew 26:53). In John 17:19 on page 40, Jesus said that he would sanctify himself or set himself apart as the sacrifice needed for the forgiveness of man's sins. This sacrifice would allow his disciples, then and now, to be made perfect, reach total harmony with Jesus and the Father, and be with Jesus in his glorified state (verses 20-24). The prayer recorded in John 17:1-26 displays a love for God and for us that is staggering. Faced with a scourging or whipping so brutal that it would leave some of his bones exposed (Psalm 22:17), faced with crucifixion or impalement on a cross or stake where he would continually struggle to breathe and be in constant, excruciating pain, Jesus' thoughts focused on God, on God's plan and on us. See the NOTE in Table 4 on page 41 for further explanation.			1. THESE words spake Jesus, and lifted up his eyes to heaven, and said, Father, the hour is come; glorify thy Son, that thy Son also may glorify thee: 2. As thou hast given him power over all flesh, that he should give eternal life to as many as thou hast given him. 3. And this is life eternal, that they might know thee the only true God, and Jesus Christ, whom thou hast sent. 4. I have glorified thee on the earth: I have finished the work which thou gavest me to do. 5. And now, O Father, glorify thou me with thine own self with the glory which I had with thee before the world was.

Table 4 (continued)

Matthew 26	Mark 14	Luke 22	John 17:6-12
			6. I have manifested thy name unto the men which thou gavest me out of the world: thine they were, and thou gavest them me; and they have kept thy word.
			7. Now they have known that all things whatsoever thou hast given me are of thee.
			8. For I have given unto them the words which thou gavest me; and they have received them, and have known surely that I came out from thee, and they have believed that thou didst send me.
			9. I pray for them: I pray not for the world, but for them which thou hast given me; for they are thine.
			10. And all mine are thine, and thine are mine; and I am glorified in them.
			11. And now I am no more in the world, but these are in the world, and I come to thee. Holy Father, keep through thine own name those whom thou hast given me, that they may be one, as we are.
			12. While I was with them in the world, I kept them in thy name: those that thou gavest me I have kept, and none of them is

Table 4 (continued)			
Matthew 26	Mark 14	Luke 22	John 17:12-21
			lost, but the son of perdition; that the scripture might be fulfilled.
			13. And now come I to thee; and these things I speak in the world, that they might have my joy fulfilled in themselves.
			14. I have given them thy word; and the world hath hated them, because they are not of the world, even as I am not of the world.
			15. I pray not that thou shouldest take them out of the world, but that thou shouldest keep them from the evil.
			16. They are not of the world, even as I am not of the world.
			17. Sanctify them through thy truth: thy word is truth.
			18. As thou hast sent me into the world, even so have I also sent them into the world.
			19. And for their sakes I sanctify myself, that they also might be sanctified through the truth.
			20. Neither pray I for these alone, but for them also which shall believe on me through their word;
			21. That they all may be one; as thou, Father, art in me, and I in thee, that they also may be one in us: that the world may believe

Matthew 26:45	Mark 14:41	Luke 22	John 17:21-26; 18:1
			that thou hast sent me.
			22. And the glory which thou gavest me I have given them; that they may be one, even as we are one:
			23. I in them, and thou in me, that they may be made perfect in one; and that the world may know that thou hast sent me, and hast loved them, as thou hast loved me.
			24. Father, I will that they also, whom thou hast given me, be with me where I am; that they may behold my glory, which thou hast given me: for thou lovedst me before the foundation of the world.
			25. O righteous Father, the world hath not known
NOTE: Between the time Jesus finished his third prayer (John 18:1 first part) and the time he crossed the brook (John 18:1 last part on page 42), he returned to his sleeping disciples and told them, "Sleep on now, and take your rest" (Matthew 26:45 first part and Mark 14:41 first part). After allowing them to sleep for some period of time, Jesus said, "It is enough (meaning 'you have slept enough'), the hour is come; behold, the Son of man is betrayed into the hands of sinners. Rise up, let us go" (Mark 14:41-42, Matthew 26:45-46). After Jesus and the disciples crossed the brook and entered a garden (John 18:1 last part), Jesus said his betrayer was at hand just as Judas and the band of men arrived (Matthew 26:46-47, Mark 14:42-43, Luke 22:47, John 18:2-3 on page 42).			thee: but I have known thee, and these have known that thou hast sent me.
			26. And I have declared unto them thy name, and will declare it: that the love wherewith thou hast loved me may be in them, and I in them.
			1. WHEN Jesus had spoken these words,
45. Then cometh he to his disciples, and saith unto them,	41. And he cometh the third time, and saith unto them,		

Table 4 (continued)			
Matthew 26:45-47	Mark 14:41-43	Luke 22:47	John 18:1-3
<u>Sleep on now</u>, and take your rest:	<u>Sleep on now</u>, and take your rest:		
	it is enough,		
behold, the hour is at hand, and the Son of man is betrayed into the hands of sinners.	the hour is come; behold, the Son of man is betrayed into the hands of sinners.		
46. <u>Rise</u>, <u>let us be going</u>:	42. <u>Rise up</u>, <u>let us go</u>;		
			he <u>went forth</u> with his disciples over the brook Cedron, where was a garden, into the which he entered, and his disciples.
			2. And Judas also, which betrayed him, knew the place: for Jesus ofttimes resorted thither with his disciples.
behold, he is at hand that doth betray me.	lo, he that betrayeth me is at hand.		
47. And while he yet spake,	43. And immediately, while he yet spake,	47. And while he yet spake,	
lo, <u>Judas</u>, one of the twelve, <u>came</u>, and with him a great multitude with swords and staves, from the chief priests and elders of the people.	<u>cometh Judas</u>, one of the twelve, and with him a great multitude with swords and staves, from the chief priests and the scribes and the elders.	<u>behold</u> a multitude, and he that was called <u>Judas</u>, one of the twelve, went before them,	3. <u>Judas</u> then, having received a band of men and officers from the chief priests and Pharisees, <u>cometh</u> thither with lanterns and torches and weapons.

Chapter 5 describes what happened from the time Judas and the band of men arrived in the garden until the time Jesus, Peter and John arrived at the high priest's palace.

Chapter 5

The Betrayal

After Judas and the band of men arrived in the garden, Jesus stepped forward and spoke to them (John 18:4-8 in Table 5).

Table 5			
Matthew 26	Mark 14	Luke 22	John 18:4-9
NOTES: 1) When Jesus spoke to the band of men, Judas stood with them (John 18:5), but then came forward and betrayed (identified) Jesus with a kiss (Matthew 26:48-49, Mark 14:44-45, Luke 22:47 last part on the following page). 2) In John 18:5, the phrase "I am he," is really just "I am." The "he" is in italics and not part of the original translation. The phrase "I am" is a phrase that translates the most holy name for God in the Hebrew scriptures (Contemporary English Version of the Bible).			4. Jesus therefore, knowing all things that should come upon him, went forth, and said unto them, Whom seek ye? 5. They answered him, Jesus of Nazareth. Jesus saith unto them, I am he. And Judas also, which betrayed him, stood with them. 6. As soon then as he had said unto them, I am he, they went backward, and fell to the ground. 7. Then asked he them again, Whom seek ye? And they said, Jesus of Nazareth. 8. Jesus answered, I have told you that I am he: if therefore ye seek me, let these go their way: 9. That the saying might be fulfilled, which he spake, Of them which thou gavest me have I lost none.

Table 5 (continued)			
Matthew 26:48-51	Mark 14:44-47	Luke 22:47-51	John 18:10
48. Now he that betrayed him gave them a sign, saying, Whomsoever I shall kiss, that same is he: hold him fast.	44. And he that betrayed him had given them a token, saying, Whomsoever I shall kiss, that same is he; take him, and lead him away safely.		
49. And forthwith he came to Jesus, and said, Hail, master; and kissed him.	45. And as soon as he was come, he goeth straightway to him, and saith, Master, master; and kissed him.	and drew near unto Jesus to kiss him.	
50. And Jesus said unto him, Friend, wherefore art thou come?			
		48. But Jesus said unto him, Judas, betrayest thou the Son of man with a kiss?	
Then came they, and laid hands on Jesus, and took him.	46. And they laid their hands on him, and took him.		
		49. When they which were about him saw what would follow, they said unto him, Lord, shall we smite with the sword?	
51. And, behold, one of them which were with Jesus stretched out his hand, and drew his sword,	47. And one of them that stood by drew a sword,	50. And one of them	10. Then Simon Peter having a sword drew it,
and struck a servant of the high priest's, and smote off his ear.	and smote a servant of the high priest, and cut off his ear.	smote the servant of the high priest, and cut off his right ear.	and smote the high priest's servant, and cut off his right ear. The servant's name was Malchus.
NOTE: The phrase, "Suffer ye thus far" (Luke 22:51) is translated "No more of this" in the Revised Standard Version.		51. And Jesus answered and said, Suffer ye thus far. And he touched his ear, and healed him.	

44

Table 5 (continued)			
Matthew 26:52-56	Mark 14:48-51	Luke 22:52-53	John 18:11
52. Then said Jesus unto him, Put up again thy sword into his place: for all they that take the sword shall perish with the sword.			11. Then said Jesus unto Peter, Put up thy sword into the sheath: the cup which my Father hath given me, shall I not drink it?
53. Thinkest thou that I cannot now pray to my Father, and he shall presently give me more than twelve legions of angels? 54. But how then shall the scriptures be fulfilled, that thus it must be?			
55. In that same hour said Jesus to the multitudes, Are ye come out as against a thief with swords and staves for to take me? I sat daily with you teaching in the temple, and ye laid no hold on me.	48. And Jesus answered and said unto them, Are ye come out, as against a thief, with swords and with staves to take me? 49. I was daily with you in the temple teaching, and ye took me not:	52. Then Jesus said unto the chief priests, and captains of the temple, and the elders, which were come to him, Be ye come out, as against a thief, with swords and staves? 53. When I was daily with you in the temple, ye stretched forth no hands against me: but this is your hour, and the power of darkness.	
56. But all this was done, that the scriptures of the prophets might be fulfilled. Then all the disciples forsook him, and fled.	but the scriptures must be fulfilled. 50. And they all forsook him, and fled. 51. And there followed him a certain young man, having a linen cloth cast about his		

Table 5 (continued)			
Matthew 26:57-58	Mark 14:51-54	Luke 22:54	John 18:12-16
	naked body; and the young men laid hold on him: 52. And he left the linen cloth, and fled from them naked.		
NOTE: The word "palace" in Matthew 26:58 and John 18:15 on this page and "hall" in Luke 22:55 on page 47 are translated from the Greek word meaning "yard, as open to the wind" (Strong's Concordance, Greek Dictionary, word #833). This Greek word is translated courtyard or court in the Revised Standard and New International Versions of the Bible.			12. Then the band and the captain and officers of the Jews took Jesus, and bound him, 13. And led him away to Annas first; for he was father in law to Caiaphas, which was the high priest that same year. 14. Now Caiaphas was he, which gave counsel to the Jews, that it was expedient that one man should die for the people.
57. And they that had laid hold on Jesus led him away to Caiaphas the high priest, where the scribes and the elders were assembled.	53. And they led Jesus away to the high priest: and with him were assembled all the chief priests and the elders and the scribes.	54. Then took they him, and led him, and brought him into the high priest's house.	
58. But Peter followed him afar off	54. And Peter followed him afar off,	And Peter followed afar off.	15. And Simon Peter followed Jesus, and so did another disciple: that disciple was known unto the high priest, and went in with Jesus into the palace of the high priest.
unto the high priest's palace,			16. But Peter stood at the door without.

The events which occurred after Jesus and Peter arrived at the house of the high priest will be discussed in Chapter 6.

The Trial

After John brought Peter into the courtyard (Matthew 26:58, Mark 14:54 and John 18:16 in Table 6-1), the woman who tended the door into the courtyard asked him if he was one of Jesus' disciples. Peter said he was not (John 18:17). This was Peter's <u>first denial</u> of Jesus Christ.

Table 6-1			
Matthew 26:58	Mark 14:54	Luke 22:55	John 18:16-18
and <u>went in</u>,	even <u>into the palace</u> of the high priest:		Then went out that other disciple, which was known unto the high priest, and spake unto her that kept the door, and <u>brought in</u> <u>Peter</u>.
			17. Then saith the damsel that kept the door unto Peter, Art not thou also one of this man's disciples? He saith, <u>I am not</u>.
			FIRST DENIAL
<u>NOTE</u>: It was cold that night (John 18:18), so someone built a fire in the hall or courtyard (Luke 22:55 first part). Peter <u>stood</u>, then <u>sat</u> by the fire to warm himself and to see the end (John 18:18, Matthew 26:58 last part, Mark 14:54 last part, Luke 22:55 last part).		55. And when they had kindled a <u>fire</u> in the midst of the hall,	18. And the servants and officers <u>stood</u> there, who had made a fire of coals; for it was <u>cold</u>: and they warmed themselves: and Peter **stood** with them, and warmed himself.
and **sat** with the servants, to see the end.	and he **sat** with the servants, and warmed himself at the fire.	and were <u>set down</u> together, Peter **sat** down among them.	

Table 6-1 (continued)			
Matthew 26:59-60	Mark 14:55-57	Luke 22	John 18:19-24
			19. The high priest then <u>asked Jesus of his disciples, and of his doctrine.</u> 20. Jesus answered him, I spake openly to the world; I ever taught in the synagogue, and in the temple, whither the Jews always resort; and in secret have I said nothing. 21. Why askest thou me? ask them which heard me, what I have said unto them: behold, they know what I said. 22. And when he had thus spoken, one of the officers which stood by struck Jesus with the palm of his hand, saying, Answerest thou the high priest so? 23. Jesus answered him, If I have spoken evil, bear witness of the evil: but if well, why smitest thou me? 24. Now Annas had sent him bound unto Caiaphas the high priest.
59. Now the chief priests, and elders, and all the council, <u>sought false witness against Jesus,</u> to put him to death; 60. But found none: yea, though many false witnesses came, yet found they none. At the last came two false witnesses,	55. And the chief priests and all the council <u>sought for witness against Jesus</u> to put him to death; and found none. 56. For many bare false witness against him, but their witness agreed not together. 57. And there arose certain,		**NOTES:** 1) The questioning of Jesus by the high priest is described in John 18:19-23. 2) The trial of Jesus is described in Matthew 26:59-66 and Mark 14:55-64.

	Table 6-1 (continued)		
Matthew 26:61-65	Mark 14:57-63	Luke 22	John 18
61. And said, This fellow said, I am able to destroy the temple of God, and to build it in three days.	and bare false witness against him, saying, 58. We heard him say, I will destroy this temple that is made with hands, and within three days I will build another made without hands. 59. But neither so did their witness agree together.		<u>NOTES</u>: 1) Do Matthew 26:61 and Mark 14:58 show how the accounts of the two false witnesses did not agree (Mark 14:59)? 2) With the word "Again" in Mark 14:61, is it possible the high priest asked Jesus if he was the Son of God <u>twice</u>? Compare Matthew 26:62-63 to Mark 14:60-61.
62. And the high priest arose, and said unto him, Answerest thou nothing? what is it which these witness against thee? 63. But Jesus held his peace. And the high priest answered and said unto him, I adjure thee by the living God, that thou tell us whether thou be the Christ, the Son of God.	60. And the high priest stood up in the midst, and asked Jesus, saying, Answerest thou nothing? what is it which these witness against thee?		
	61. But he held his peace, and answered nothing. <u>Again</u> the high priest asked him, and said unto him, Art thou the Christ, the Son of the Blessed?		
64. Jesus saith unto him, Thou hast said: nevertheless I say unto you, Hereafter shall ye see the Son of man sitting on the right hand of power, and coming in the clouds of heaven.	62. And Jesus said, I am: and ye shall see the Son of man sitting on the right hand of power, and coming in the clouds of heaven.		
65. Then the high priest rent his clothes, saying, He hath spoken blasphemy;	63. Then the high priest rent his clothes, and saith,		

Table 6-1 (continued)

Matthew 26:65-70	Mark 14:63-68	Luke 22:56-57	John 18
what further need have we of witnesses? behold, now ye have heard his blasphemy. 66. What think ye? They answered and said, He is guilty of death.	What need we any further witnesses? 64. Ye have heard the blasphemy: what think ye? And they all condemned him to be guilty of death.		
67. Then did they spit in his face, and buffeted him; and others smote him with the palms of their hands, 68. Saying, Prophesy unto us, thou Christ, Who is he that smote thee?	65. And some began to spit on him, and to cover his face, and to buffet him, and to say unto him, Prophesy: and the servants did strike him with the palms of their hands.		NOTE: As Jesus was being mocked and beaten (Matthew 26:67-68, Mark 14:65), Peter sat outside and below in the courtyard by the fire (Matthew 26:69, Mark 14:66). After a maid approached Peter and stared at him, she told him that he was also with Jesus of Galilee (Matthew 26:69 last part and Mark 14:67 last part). She then told the others by the fire that Peter was with Jesus (Luke 22:56 last part). Peter told the woman he did not know Jesus and did not know nor understand what she was talking about. This was Peter's second denial (Matthew 26:70, Mark 14:68, Luke 22:57). After this denial, Peter apparently felt uncomfortable staying at the fire and went out into the porch, where he denied Jesus the third time (Mark 14:68 last part on this page, Matthew 26:71-72 on page 51).
69. Now Peter sat without (outside) in the palace: and a damsel came unto him, saying, Thou also wast with Jesus of Galilee.	66. And as Peter was beneath in the palace, there cometh one of the maids of the high priest: 67. And when she saw Peter warming himself, she looked upon him, and said, And thou also wast with Jesus of Nazareth.	56. But a certain maid beheld him as he sat by the fire, and earnestly looked upon him, and said, This man was also with him.	
70. But he denied before them all, saying, I know not what thou sayest.	68. But he denied, saying, I know not, neither understand I what thou sayest.	57. And he denied him, saying, Woman, I know him not.	
SECOND DENIAL	**SECOND DENIAL**	**SECOND DENIAL**	
	And he went out into the porch;		

Table 6-1 (continued)			
Matthew 26:71-72	Mark 14	Luke 22	John 18
71. And <u>when he was gone out into the porch</u>, another maid saw him, and said unto them that were there, This fellow was also with Jesus of Nazareth. 72. And again he <u>denied</u> with an oath, <u>I do not know the man</u>. **THIRD DENIAL**			

So far, Peter has denied Jesus three times.

FIRST DENIAL (John 18:17 in Table 6-1 on page 47): When Peter <u>stepped through the gate</u> to the courtyard, the <u>woman who tended the gate</u> asked, "Art not thou also one of this man's disciples?" Peter responded, "I am not." This denial occurred before Jesus was questioned by the high priest (John 18:19-23) and given a mock trial (Matthew 26:59-66 and Mark 14:55-64).

SECOND DENIAL (Matthew 26:70, Mark 14:68 and Luke 22:57 in Table 6-1 on page 50): After Jesus' trial, as Peter <u>sat by the fire</u>, a <u>maid</u> who was stationed in the courtyard told Peter and those sitting around the fire that Peter had been with Jesus. Peter responded that he did not know Jesus and did not know, nor understand, what the maid was talking about. <u>After</u> this second denial, Peter <u>went out into the porch</u>.

THIRD DENIAL (Matthew 26:72 in Table 6-1 above): <u>While</u> Peter was <u>on the porch</u>, <u>another maid</u> told those on the porch that Peter had been with Jesus. Peter again denied saying with an oath, "I do not know the man."

But Peter denied Jesus **more than three times!**

In fact, Peter denied Jesus <u>six times</u>, but to prove this is true, let's first see that Peter denied Jesus more than three times. This is shown in Matthew 26:71-75 below. The denial in Matthew 26:72 is Peter's <u>third</u> denial on the porch. The denial in Matthew 26:74 is the denial associated with Peter's Galilean accent and clearly occurred <u>after</u> Peter's <u>third</u> denial on the porch. Table 6-2 on page 52 clearly shows Peter denied Jesus <u>more than three times</u>!

Matthew 26:71-75
71. And when he was gone out into the <u>porch</u>, another maid saw him, and said unto them that were there, This fellow was also with Jesus of Nazareth.
72. And again he denied with an oath, <u>I do not know the man</u> (third denial in Table 6-1 above).
73. And after a while came unto him they that stood by (the fire), and said to Peter, Surely thou also art one of them; for <u>thy speech</u> (Galilean accent) bewrayeth thee.
74. Then began he to curse and to swear, saying, <u>I know not the man</u>. And immediately the cock crew.
75. And Peter remembered the word of Jesus, which said unto him, Before the cock crow, thou shalt deny me thrice. And he went out, and wept bitterly.

Table 6-2				
	Matthew	Mark	Luke	John
1)				Denial made to the woman who kept the door to the courtyard (John 18:17 p. 47).
2)	Denial made to the maid in the courtyard as Peter sat by the fire (Matthew 26:70 p. 50).	Denial made to the maid in the courtyard as Peter sat by the fire (Mark 14:68 p. 50).	Denial made to the maid in the courtyard as Peter sat by the fire (Luke 22:57 p. 50).	
3)	Denial made to a different maid on the porch (Matthew 26:72 p. 51).			
4)	Denial associated with Peter's Galilean accent (Matt. 26:74 p. 51).			

Now let's look at the denial described in Mark 14:70 below. This denial occurred after Peter's second denial (Mark 14:68), but before the denial associated with Peter's Galilean accent (Mark 14:71).

Mark 14:66-72
66. And as Peter was beneath in the palace, there cometh one of the maids of the high priest:
67. And when she saw Peter warming himself, she looked upon him, and said, And thou also wast with Jesus of Nazareth.
68. But he denied, saying, I know not, neither understand I what thou sayest (second denial on page 50). And he went out into the porch; and the cock crew.
69. And a maid saw him again, and began to say to them that stood by (the fire), This is one of them.
70. And he denied it again. And a little after, they that stood by said again to Peter, Surely thou art one of them: for thou art a Galilean, and thy speech agreeth thereto.
71. But he began to curse and to swear, saying, I know not this man of whom ye speak.
72. And the second time the cock crew . . .

The rooster crowing that occurred after the denial associated with Peter's Galilean accent was actually the second time the rooster crowed (Mark 14:70-72). The first time is shown in Mark 14:68. Therefore since the rooster crowing in Matthew 26:74 on page 51 occurred after the denial associated with Peter's Galilean accent, it was also the second time the rooster crowed (Matthew 26:73-74). The first time the rooster crowed is not recorded in Matthew.

Mark 14:69 above describes the second time the maid stationed in the courtyard saw Peter by the fire and the second time she told those gathered by the fire that Peter was Jesus' disciple. The first time she saw Peter and made this same accusation is described in Matthew 26:69, Mark 14:66-67 and Luke 22:56 in Table 6-1 on page 50. So, the denial in Mark 14:70 is another denial made to the maid stationed in the courtyard (see denial 4 in Table 6-3 on page 53).

Now notice how denial 4 differs from denial 3 in Table 6-3. Denial 4 was made to the maid stationed in the courtyard, while denial 3 was made to "another maid" stationed on the porch (Matthew 26:71-72 on page 51).

It is very important that you understand that denial 2 and denial 4 in Table 6-3 were made to the maid stationed in the courtyard at different times. Denial 3 was made to a totally different maid stationed on the porch.

Table 6-3				
	Matthew	Mark	Luke	John
1)				Denial made to the woman who kept the door to the courtyard (John 18:17 p. 47).
2)	Denial made to the maid in the courtyard as Peter sat by the fire (Matthew 26:70 p. 50).	Denial made to the maid in the courtyard as Peter sat by the fire (Mark 14:68 p. 50).	Denial made to the maid in the courtyard as Peter sat by the fire (Luke 22:57 p. 50).	
3)	Denial made to a different maid on the porch (Matthew 26:72 p. 51).			
		Cock crows the first time (Mark 14:68 p. 52).		
4)		Another denial made to the same maid in the courtyard by the fire (Mark 14:70 first part p. 52).		
5)	Denial associated with Peter's Galilean accent (Matthew 26:74 on p. 51).	Denial associated with Peter's Galilean accent (Mark 14:71 p. 52).		
	Cock crows the (second) time (Matt. 26:74 p. 51).	Cock crows the second time (Mark 14:72 p. 52).		

That Peter came back into the courtyard after his third denial on the porch is shown in Matthew 26:71-75 on page 51. Notice the words "gone out" in verse 71 and "went out" in verse 75. Matthew 26:71-72 shows that after Peter was "gone out" into the porch, he denied Jesus the third time. After the denial associated with his Galilean accent (verse 74), Peter went out or left the courtyard again (verse 75). So, between the time Peter denied Jesus on the porch (verse 72) and the time he denied Jesus in verse 74, Peter went back into the courtyard.

The denial in Luke 22:58 on page 54 is different from every denial we've discussed so far. This denial occurred after Peter's second denial (Luke 22:57), but before the denial associated with Peter's Galilean accent (Luke 22:60).

Luke 22:55-60
55. And when they had kindled a fire in the midst of the hall (courtyard), and were set down together, Peter sat down among them.

56. But a certain maid beheld him as he sat by the fire, and earnestly looked upon him, and said, This man was also with him.

57. And he denied him, saying, <u>Woman</u>, <u>I know him not</u> (second denial on page 50).

58. And after a little while another saw him, and said, Thou art also of them. And Peter said, <u>Man</u>, <u>I am not</u>.

59. And about the space of one hour after another confidently affirmed, saying, Of a truth this fellow also was with him: for he is a <u>Galilaean</u>.

60. And Peter said, <u>Man</u>, <u>I know not what thou sayest</u>. And immediately, while he yet spake, the cock crew.

Since the cock crowing in verse 60 occurred after the denial associated with Peter's Galilean accent, it is actually the second time the cock crew. As with Matthew, the first time the cock crew is not recorded in Luke.

The denial in Luke 22:58
*   Is not Peter's first or second denial because it occurred after Peter's second denial (Luke 22:57).
*   Is not Peter's third denial (Matthew 26:71-72 on page 51). The denial in Luke 22:58 was made to a <u>lone male</u> while the third denial was made to a <u>maid</u> and <u>others</u> on the porch.
*   Is not denial 4 in Table 6-3 on page 53. Again, the denial in Luke 22:58 was made to a <u>lone male</u> while denial 4 in Table 6-3 was made to a <u>maid</u> and <u>others</u> by the fire in the courtyard (Mark 14:69-70 on page 52).

The three denials described in Luke 22:55-60 are shown in Table 6-4 on page 55. That denials 4 and 5 in Table 6-4 occurred in the order shown will be discussed in more detail later. Denial 4 and denial 6 in Table 6-4 are further described in John 18:16-27.

John 18:16-27
16. But Peter stood at the door without. Then went out that other disciple, which was known unto the high priest, and spake unto her that kept the door, and brought in Peter.

17. Then saith the damsel that kept the door unto Peter, Art not thou also one of this man's disciples? He saith, <u>I am not</u> (first denial on page 47).

18. And the servants and officers stood there, who had made a fire of coals; for it was cold: and they warmed themselves: and Peter stood with them, and warmed himself.

19. The high priest then asked Jesus of his disciples, and of his doctrine.

20. Jesus answered him, I spake openly to the world; I ever taught in the synagogue, and in the temple, whither the Jews always resort; and in secret have I said nothing.

21. Why askest thou me? ask them which heard me, what I have said unto them: behold, they know what I said.

22. And when he had thus spoken, one of the officers which stood by struck Jesus with the palm of his hand, saying, Answerest thou the high priest so?

23. Jesus answered him, If I have spoken evil, bear witness of the evil: but if well, why smitest thou me?

24. Now Annas had sent him bound unto Caiaphas the high priest.

25. And Simon Peter stood and warmed himself (by the fire). They said therefore unto him, Art not thou also one of his disciples? <u>He denied it</u>, and said, <u>I am not</u>.

26. One of the servants of the high priest, being his kinsman whose ear Peter cut off, saith, Did not I see thee in the garden with him?

27. Peter then <u>denied again</u>: and immediately the cock crew.

The denial in John 18:25
*   Is not Peter's first denial because it occurred <u>after</u> his first denial (verse 17).

* Is not his second denial (Matthew 26:70, Mark 14:68 and Luke 22:57 on page 50). The second denial was made as Peter <u>sat</u> by the fire. The denial in John 18:25 was made as Peter <u>stood</u> by the fire.
* Is not Peter's third denial (Matthew 26:71-72 on page 51). The third denial was made to a maid and others <u>on the porch</u>, while the denial in John 18:25 was made <u>in the courtyard</u> by the fire.

Denial 4 in Table 6-4 (Mark 14:70 first part) was made to a maid <u>by the fire</u> in the courtyard. The denial in John 18:25 was made as Peter stood <u>by the fire</u> in the courtyard. As I will explain shortly, the denial described in John 18:25 and the denial described in Mark 14:70 first part are the <u>same</u> denial. I will also explain how the denial described in John 18:26-27 is the denial associated with Peter's Galilean accent.

Table 6-4				
	Matthew	Mark	Luke	John
1)				Denial made to the woman who kept the door to the courtyard (John 18:17 p. 47).
2)	Denial made to the <u>maid</u> in the <u>courtyard</u> as Peter <u>sat</u> by the fire (Matthew 26:70 p. 50)	Denial made to the <u>maid</u> in the <u>courtyard</u> as Peter <u>sat</u> by the fire (Mark 14:68 p. 50).	Denial made to the <u>maid</u> in the <u>courtyard</u> as Peter <u>sat</u> by the fire (Luke 22:57 p. 50).	
3)	Denial made to a <u>different maid</u> on the <u>porch</u> (Matthew 26:72 p. 51).			
		Cock crows first time (Mark 14:68 p. 52).		
4)		<u>Another</u> denial made to the <u>same</u> maid in the <u>courtyard</u> by the fire (Mark 14:70 first part p. 52).		Denial made as Peter <u>stood</u> in the <u>courtyard</u> by the fire (John 18:25 p. 54).
5)			Denial made to a <u>lone male</u> (Luke 22:58 p. 54).	
6)	Denial associated with Peter's <u>Galilean accent</u> (Matthew 26:74 p. 51).	Denial associated with Peter's <u>Galilean accent</u> (Mark 14:71 p. 52).	Denial associated with Peter's <u>Galilean accent</u> (Luke 22:60 p. 54).	Denial associated with Peter's <u>Galilean accent</u> (John 18:27 p. 54).
	Cock crows the (second) time (Matt. 26:74 p. 51).	Cock crows the <u>second</u> time (Mark 14:72 p. 52).	Cock crows the (second) time (Luke 22:60 p. 54)	Cock crows the (second) time (John 18:27 p. 54)

Table 6-4 shows that Peter denied Jesus six times - three times before the rooster crowed the first time and three more times before the rooster crowed the second time. And this is <u>exactly</u> what Jesus said Peter would do! See Table 6-5 on page 56. The scriptures shown in Table 6-5 are the same scriptures shown on page 35 in Table 4.

Table 6-5			
Matthew 26:31-34	Mark 14:27-30	Luke 22	John 16
31. Then saith Jesus unto them, All ye shall be <u>offended</u> because of me this night: for it is written, I will smite the shepherd, and the sheep of the flock shall be scattered abroad. 32. But after I am risen again, I will go before you into Galilee. 33. Peter answered and said unto him, Though all men shall be offended because of thee, yet <u>will I never be offended</u>. 34. Jesus said unto him, Verily I say unto thee, That this night, <u>before the cock crow</u>, <u>thou shalt deny me thrice</u>.	27. And Jesus saith unto them, All ye shall be <u>offended</u> because of me this night: for it is written, I will smite the shepherd, and the sheep shall be scattered. 28. But after that I am risen, I will go before you into Galilee. 29. But Peter said unto him, Although all shall be offended, yet will not I. 30. And Jesus saith unto him, Verily I say unto thee, That this day, even in this night, <u>before the cock crow</u> **twice,** <u>thou shalt deny me thrice</u>.		<u>**NOTES:**</u> 1) After Jesus said all the disciples would be offended, Peter said he wouldn't (Matthew 26:31,33, Mark 14:27). Jesus then told Peter that he would deny him three times before the rooster crowed (Matthew 26:34). 2) When Peter continued to argue (Mark 14:29), Jesus <u>added</u> the prophecy in Mark 14:30 that Peter would deny him three (more) times before the rooster crowed <u>twice</u>. "Twice" means twice (Strong's Concordance, Greek Dictionary, word #1364). 3) Jesus' statement in Matthew 26:34 was made after Jesus and the disciples <u>left</u> the goodman's house (Matthew 26: 30 p. 26) and is a restatement of the prophecy Jesus made earlier <u>in</u> the goodman's house (Luke 22:34, John 18:38 p. 21).

There is <u>no way</u> Jesus said Peter would deny him <u>just</u> three times! Table 6-4 on page 55 shows six <u>different</u> denials. Jesus predicted Peter would deny him three times before the rooster crowed (the first time) and three (more) times before the rooster crowed the second time. And Peter did <u>exactly</u> what Jesus said he would do!

After Peter's third denial, while Peter was still on the porch, the rooster crowed the first time (Mark 14:68 last part in Table 6-6 page 58). Peter probably felt uncomfortable staying on the porch after his third denial, so he returned to the courtyard where he <u>stood</u> by the fire <u>again</u> to warm himself (John 18:25 first part). Remember, it was cold on the porch (John 18:18 page 47). The first time Peter stood by the fire was shortly after he originally entered the courtyard (John 18:18 page 47). Peter sat by the fire during Jesus' questioning and trial and remained seated until he went out into the porch (Matthew 26:58-70, Mark 14:54-68, Luke 22:55-57, pages 47-50).

As he stood by the fire, he was seen by the same maid who had seen him earlier that evening sitting by the fire (Mark 14:69 page 58). After the maid told the people gathered by the fire that Peter was one of Jesus' disciples, the people asked Peter, "Aren't you also one of his disciples?" (John 18:25 middle part). Peter said he wasn't. Mark 14:70 first part and John 18:25 last part describe Peter's fourth denial. A little later, a lone male told Peter, "You are also one of them." Peter responded, "Man, I am not" (Luke 22:58 page 58). This was Peter's fifth denial.

Prior to Peter's sixth denial, the people who had earlier stood by the fire came to Peter and twice told him he was one of Jesus' disciples because of his accent (Matthew 26:73 page 58, Mark 14:70 last part page 59. Also see NOTE on page 59). Then a man in this group asked Peter, "Didn't I see you in the garden with him?" (John 18:26). John identifies this man as one of the servants of the high priest. I believe Luke describes this same man as just "another" member of this group (Luke 22:59 last part page 59). So, after this man asked Peter if he had seen him in the garden, he realized that he had seen Peter in the garden and could boldly state, "Of a truth this fellow also was with him: for he is a Galilaean."

After Peter's sixth denial, the rooster crowed (Matthew 26:74 last part, Mark 14:72 first part, Luke 22:60 last part, John 18:27 last part). As previously discussed, Matthew, Luke and John say only that the rooster crowed; Mark identifies this crowing as the second time the rooster crowed. After the rooster crowed the second time, Jesus turned and looked at Peter, and Peter remembered that Jesus had said, "Before the rooster crows, you will deny me three times." Peter then left the courtyard and wept bitterly (Luke 22:61-62, Matthew 26:75). As he wept, Peter remembered that Jesus had also said, "Before the rooster crows twice, you will deny me three times," and continued to weep (Mark 14:72 last part page 60).

The study of Peter's denials requires a lot of thought and effort. But I believe that if you study the gospels thoroughly, you will believe, as I do, that the only way all of the scriptures related to Peter's denials of Jesus Christ can agree is for the events to have occurred as shown in Tables 6-1 and 6-6.

A summary of the six denials follows.

FIRST DENIAL (John 18:17 on page 47): When Peter stepped through the gate to the courtyard, the woman who tended the gate asked Peter if he was one of Jesus' disciples. Peter said he wasn't.

SECOND DENIAL (Matthew 26:70, Mark 14:68 and Luke 22:57 on page 50): After Jesus' trial, as Peter sat by the fire, the maid who was stationed in the courtyard told Peter, and then told those sitting around Peter at the fire, that Peter was with Jesus. Peter denied it. After this second denial, Peter went out into the porch.

THIRD DENIAL (Matthew 26:72 on page 58): While Peter was on the porch, another maid told those on the porch that Peter was with Jesus. Peter denied it and the rooster crowed the first time.

FOURTH DENIAL (Mark 14:70 first part and John 18:25 last part on page 58): After the rooster crowed the first time, Peter returned to the courtyard from the porch and stood by the fire again to warm himself. A maid, who had seen him earlier, told those standing by the fire that Peter was one of Jesus' disciples. Those standing by the fire then asked Peter if he was one of Jesus' disciples. Peter said he was not.

FIFTH DENIAL (Luke 22:58 on page 58): While Peter was in the courtyard he was seen by a lone male who said, "You are also one of them." Peter responded, "Man, I am not."

	Table 6-6		
Matthew 26:71-73	Mark 14:68-70	Luke 22:58-59	John 18:25
	68. . . . And he went out into the porch.		**NOTE**: Mark 14:68 last part and Matthew 26:71-72 from Table 6-1 on pages 50 and 51 are repeated in this table for ease of reading.
71. And when he was gone out into the porch, another maid saw him, and said unto them that were there, This fellow was also with Jesus of Nazareth.			
72. And again he <u>denied</u> with an oath, <u>I do not know the man</u>.			
THIRD DENIAL			
	and <u>the cock crew</u>.		
			25. And Simon Peter <u>stood</u> and <u>warmed himself</u>.
	69. And a maid saw him <u>again</u>, and began to say to them that stood by, This is one of them.		
			They said therefore unto him, Art not thou also one of his disciples? He <u>denied it</u>, and said,
	70. And he <u>denied it again</u>.		<u>I am not</u>.
	FOURTH DENIAL		**FOURTH DENIAL**
		58. And after a little while another saw him, and said, <u>Thou art also of them</u>. And Peter said, <u>Man</u>, <u>I am not</u>.	
		FIFTH DENIAL	
73. And after a while came unto him they that stood by, and said to Peter, Surely thou also art one of them; for <u>thy speech bewrayeth thee</u>.	And a little after,	59. And about the space of one hour after	

58

	Table 6-6 (continued)		
Matthew 26:74-75	Mark 14:70-72	Luke 22:59-62	John 18:26-27
NOTE: The word "again" in Mark 14:70 shows that the people told Peter he was Jesus' disciple because of his accent <u>twice</u> (see also Matthew 26:73 p. 58).	they that stood by said <u>again</u> to Peter, Surely thou art one of them: for <u>thou art a Galilaean</u>, and <u>thy speech agreeth thereto</u>.		
			26. One of the servants of the high priest, being his kinsman whose ear Peter cut off, saith, Did not I <u>see thee</u> in the garden with him?
		another <u>confidently affirmed</u>, saying, <u>Of a truth</u> this fellow also was with him: for <u>he is a Galilaean</u>.	
		60. And Peter said, Man, <u>I know not what thou sayest</u>.	
74. Then began he to curse and to swear, saying, <u>I know not the man</u>.	71. But he began to curse and to swear, saying, <u>I know not this man of whom ye speak</u>.		27. Peter then <u>denied again</u>:
SIXTH DENIAL	SIXTH DENIAL	SIXTH DENIAL	SIXTH DENIAL
And immediately the cock crew.	72. And the second time the cock crew.	And immediately, while he yet spake, the cock crew.	and immediately the cock crew.
		61. And the Lord turned, and looked upon Peter.	
75. And <u>Peter remembered</u> the word of Jesus, which said unto him, <u>Before the cock crow</u>, thou shalt deny me thrice.		And <u>Peter remembered</u> the word of the Lord, how he had said unto him, <u>Before the cock crow</u>, thou shalt deny me thrice.	
And he went out, and <u>wept bitterly</u>.		62. And Peter went out, and <u>wept bitterly</u>.	

Table 6-6 (continued)			
Matthew 26	Mark 14:72	Luke 22	John 18
	And <u>Peter called to mind</u> the word that Jesus said unto him, <u>Before the cock crow twice</u>, thou shalt deny me thrice. And when he thought thereon, he <u>wept</u>.		

SIXTH DENIAL (Matthew 26:74 first part, Mark 14:71, Luke 22:60 first part and John 18:27 first part on page 59): After a series of conversations regarding Peter's Galilean accent, an individual confidently affirmed to those gathered with Peter, "Of a truth this fellow was also with him." Peter replied, "Man, I don't know what you're talking about," and then began to curse and swear that he did not know Jesus Christ. Immediately, while he spoke, <u>the rooster crowed the second time</u>.

Table 6-7 shows how Peter's six denials are recorded in the gospels.

Table 6-7			
Matthew	Mark	Luke	John
			FIRST DENIAL John 18:17
SECOND DENIAL Matthew 26:70	**SECOND DENIAL** Mark 14:68	**SECOND DENIAL** Luke 22:57	
THIRD DENIAL Matthew 26:72			
	FOURTH DENIAL Mark 14:70		**FOURTH DENIAL** John 18:25
		FIFTH DENIAL Luke 22:58	
SIXTH DENIAL Matthew 26:74	**SIXTH DENIAL** Mark 14:71	**SIXTH DENIAL** Luke 22:60	**SIXTH DENIAL** John 18:27

Isn't it interesting that each gospel contains three denials?

Chapter 7

Pilate

As Peter wept outside (Mark 14:72 in Table 6-6 on page 60), Jesus was mocked and beaten (Luke 22:63-65 in Table 7). As soon as it was day, Jesus was brought before the council, questioned and led to Pilate to be put to death (Matthew 27:1-2; Mark 15:1; Luke 22:66-71, 23:1; and John 18:28).

Table 7			
Matthew 27:1	Mark 15:1	Luke 22:63-68	John 18
		63. And the men that held Jesus mocked him, and smote him. 64. And when they had blindfolded him, they struck him on the face, and asked him, saying, Prophesy, who is it that smote thee? 65. And many other things blasphemously spake they against him.	
1. WHEN the morning was come, all the chief priests and elders of the people took counsel against Jesus to put him to death:	1. AND straightway in the morning the chief priests held a consultation with the elders and scribes and the whole council,	66. And as soon as it was day, the elders of the people and the chief priests and the scribes came together, and led him into their council, saying, 67. Art thou the Christ? tell us. And he said unto them, If I tell you, ye will not believe: 68. And if I also ask you, ye will not answer me, nor let me go.	

Table 7 (continued)			
Matthew 27:2-6	Mark 15:1	Luke 22:69-71; 23:1	John 18:28
		69. Hereafter shall the Son of man sit on the right hand of the power of God. 70. Then said they all, Art thou then the Son of God? And he said unto them, Ye say that I am. 71. And they said, What need we any further witness? for we ourselves have heard of his own mouth.	
2. And when they had bound him, they led him away, and delivered him to Pontius Pilate the governor.	and bound Jesus, and carried him away, and delivered him to Pilate.	1. AND the whole multitude of them arose, and led him unto Pilate.	28. Then led they Jesus from Caiaphas unto the hall of judgment: and it was early;
3. Then Judas, which had betrayed him, when he saw that he was condemned, repented himself, and brought again the thirty pieces of silver to the chief priests and elders, 4. Saying, I have sinned in that I have betrayed the innocent blood. And they said, What is that to us? see thou to that. 5. And he cast down the pieces of silver in the temple, and departed, and went and hanged himself. 6. And the chief priests took the silver pieces, and said, It is not lawful for to put them into			and they themselves went not into the judgment hall, lest they should be defiled; but that they might eat the passover.

Table 7 (continued)

Matthew 27:6-10	Mark 15	Luke 23	John 18:29-31
the treasury, because it is the price of blood. 7. And they took counsel, and bought with them the potter's field, to bury strangers in. 8. Wherefore that field was called, The field of blood, unto this day. 9. Then was fulfilled that which was spoken by Jeremy the prophet, saying, And they took the thirty pieces of silver, the price of him that was valued, whom they of the children of Israel did value; 10. And gave them for the potter's field, as the Lord appointed me.			
NOTE: At the judgment hall, Pilate went out and asked the Jews what accusation they brought against Jesus. When the Jews responded that Jesus had said he was a king, Pilate entered the judgment hall and asked Jesus if he was King of the Jews (John 18:29-33, Luke 23:2-3, Mark 15:2, Matthew 27:11). Pilate was satisfied with Jesus' statements and told the Jews he found no fault in Jesus. They became very angry and accused Jesus of many things (John 18:34-38, Matthew 27:11-12, Mark 15:2-3, Luke 23:3-5).			29. Pilate then <u>went out</u> unto them, and said, <u>What accusation</u> bring ye against this man? 30. They answered and said unto him, If he were not a malefactor, we would not have delivered him up unto thee. 31. Then said Pilate unto them, Take ye him, and judge him according to your law. The Jews therefore said unto him, It is not lawful for us to put any man to death:

	Table 7 (continued)		
Matthew 27:11	Mark 15:2	Luke 23:2-3	John 18:32-36
			32. That the saying of Jesus might be fulfilled, which he spake, signifying what death he should die.
		2. And they began to accuse him, saying, We found this fellow perverting the nation, and forbidding to give tribute to Caesar, saying that he himself is Christ a King.	
11. And Jesus stood before the governor:			33. Then Pilate entered into the judgment hall again, and called Jesus,
and the governor asked him, saying, Art thou the King of the Jews?	2. And Pilate asked him, Art thou the King of the Jews?	3. And Pilate asked him, saying, Art thou the King of the Jews?	and said unto him, Art thou the King of the Jews?
			34. Jesus answered him, Sayest thou this thing of thyself, or did others tell it thee of me?
			35. Pilate answered, Am I a Jew? Thine own nation and the chief priests have delivered thee unto me: what hast thou done?
			36. Jesus answered, My kingdom is not of this world: if my kingdom were of this world, then would my servants fight, that I should not be delivered to the Jews: but now is my kingdom not from hence.

Table 7 (continued)			
Matthew 27:11-14	Mark 15:2-3	Luke 23:3-5	John 18:37-38
			37. Pilate therefore said unto him, Art thou a king then?
And Jesus said unto him, Thou sayest.	And he answering said unto him, Thou sayest it.	And he answered him and said, Thou sayest it.	Jesus answered, Thou sayest that I am a King. To this end was I born, and for this cause came I into the world, that I should bear witness unto the truth. Every one that is of the truth heareth my voice. 38. Pilate saith unto him, What is truth? And when he had said this, he went out again unto the Jews,
		4. Then said Pilate to the chief priests and to the people, I find no fault in this man. 5. And they were the more fierce, saying, He stirreth up the people, teaching throughout all Jewry, beginning from Galilee to this place.	and saith unto them, I find in him no fault at all.
12. And when he was accused of the chief priests and elders, he answered nothing.	3. And the chief priests accused him of many things: but he answered nothing.		
13. Then said Pilate unto him, Hearest thou not how many things they witness against thee? 14. And he answered him to never a word; insomuch that the governor marvelled greatly.			

Table 7 (continued)			
Matthew 27	Mark 15:4-5	Luke 23:6-12	John 18
	4. And Pilate asked him <u>again</u>, saying, Answerest thou nothing? behold how many things they witness against thee. 5. But Jesus yet <u>answered nothing</u>; so that Pilate marvelled.		
<u>NOTE</u>: After Pilate sent Jesus to Herod, Herod sent him back to Pilate (Luke 23:7,11).		6. When Pilate heard of Galilee, he asked whether the man were a Galilaean. 7. And as soon as he knew that he belonged unto Herod's jurisdiction, <u>he sent him to Herod</u>, who himself also was at Jerusalem at that time. 8. And when Herod saw Jesus, he was exceeding glad: for he was desirous to see him of a long season, because he had heard many things of him; and he hoped to have seen some miracle done by him. 9. Then he questioned with him in many words; but he answered him nothing. 10. And the chief priests and scribes stood and vehemently accused him. 11. And Herod with his men of war set him at nought, and mocked him, and arrayed him in a gorgeous robe, and <u>sent him again to Pilate</u>. 12. And the same day Pilate and Herod	

Table 7 (continued)			
Matthew 27:15-18	Mark 15:6-11	Luke 23:12-13	John 18:39
		were made friends together: for before they were at enmity between them-selves.	
15. Now at that feast the governor was wont to release unto the people a prisoner, whom they would. 16. And they had then a notable prisoner, called Barabbas.	6. Now at that feast he released unto them one prisoner, whomsoever they desired. 7. And there was one named Barabbas, which lay bound with them that had made insurrection with him, who had committed murder in the insurrection. 8. And the multitude crying aloud began to desire him to do as he had ever done unto them.		**NOTE**: This "trial" was taking place during the Jewish passover season and it was traditional for Pilate to release one prisoner to the Jews. Therefore, after Jesus was returned from Herod, Pilate's next attempt to free Jesus was to ask the crowd of Jews whom Pilate should release, Barabbas or Jesus (Matthew 27:15-18, Mark 15:6-10, Luke 23:13). When the people chose Barabbas, Pilate said Jesus had done nothing worthy of death, so he would chastise or scourge Jesus and then release him (Mark 15:11, John 18:39-40, Luke 23:14-17). This _first_ scourging in John 19:1 was an attempt by Pilate to appease the Jews and still release Jesus alive.
17. Therefore when they were <u>gathered together</u>, Pilate said unto them, Whom will ye that I release unto you? Barabbas, or Jesus which is called Christ?		13. And Pilate, when he had <u>called together</u> the chief priests and the rulers and the people,	
	9. But Pilate answered them, saying, Will ye that I release unto you the King of the Jews? 10. For he knew that the chief priests had delivered him for envy.		
18. For he knew that for envy they had delivered him.			
	11. But the chief priests moved the people, that he should rather <u>release Barabbas</u> unto them.		
			39. But ye have a custom, that I

Table 7 (continued)			
Matthew 27:19-20	Mark 15	Luke 23:14-17	John 18:39-40; 19:1-3
NOTES: 1) With the word "again" does John 18:40 describe the <u>second</u> time the Jews said to release Barabbas? Is the <u>first</u> time described in Mark 15:11 on page 67? 2) Did Pilate sit in the judgment seat to sentence Jesus to be scourged (Matthew 27:19)? Pilate scourged Jesus in the hope of releasing him, but while Jesus was being scourged did the chief priests and elders persuade the people to release Barabbas and execute Jesus (John 19:1-3, Matthew 27:19-20)?		14. Said unto them, Ye have brought this man unto me, as one that perverteth the people: and, behold, I, having examined him before you, have found no fault in this man touching those things whereof ye accuse him: 15. No, nor yet Herod: for I sent you to him; and, lo, nothing worthy of death is done unto him. 16. I will therefore <u>chastise him</u>, and <u>release him</u>. 17. (For of necessity he must release one unto them at the feast.)	should release unto you one at the passover: will ye therefore that I release unto you the King of the Jews? 40. Then cried they all again, saying, Not this man, but Barabbas. Now Barabbas was a robber.
19. When he was set down on the judgment seat, his wife sent unto him, saying, Have thou nothing to do with that just man: for I have suffered many things this day in a dream because of him. 20. But the chief priests and elders persuaded the multitude that they should ask			1. THEN Pilate therefore took Jesus, and <u>scourged him</u>. 2. And the soldiers plaited a crown of thorns, and put it on his head, and they put on him a purple robe, 3. And said, Hail, King of the Jews! and they smote him with their hands.

Table 7 (continued)			
Matthew 27:20	Mark 15	Luke 23	John 19:4-10
Barabbas, and destroy Jesus.			
NOTES: 1) After the scourging, a terrible punishment by itself, Pilate brought Jesus before the crowd and declared he found no fault in Jesus (John 19:4-5). The chief priests and officers cried out to crucify him, but Pilate continued to argue that he found no fault worthy of a death sentence. But the Jews had a more serious charge they had not brought up before: they claimed that Jesus had made himself the Son of God. At this charge Pilate became even more afraid (John 19:6-8). Apparently the warning from his wife in Matthew 27:19 on page 68 had already frightened him. 2) When Pilate asked Jesus where he came from and Jesus did not respond, Pilate threatened him. The internal strength exhibited by Jesus when he told Pilate that he could do nothing to him that God didn't allow must have frightened Pilate badly, for Pilate tried desperately to release Jesus (John 19:9-12).			4. Pilate therefore went forth again, and saith unto them, Behold, I bring him forth to you, that ye may know that I find no fault in him. 5. Then came Jesus forth, wearing the crown of thorns, and the purple robe. And Pilate saith unto them, Behold the man! 6. When the chief priests therefore and officers saw him, they cried out, saying, Crucify him, crucify him. Pilate saith unto them, Take ye him, and crucify him: for I find no fault in him. 7. The Jews answered him, We have a law, and by our law he ought to die, because <u>he made himself the Son of God</u>. 8. When Pilate therefore heard that saying, he was the <u>more afraid</u>; 9. And went again into the judgment hall, and saith unto Jesus, <u>Whence art thou</u>? But Jesus gave him no answer. 10. Then saith Pilate unto him, Speakest thou not unto me? knowest thou not that I have power to crucify thee, and

Table 7 (continued)

Matthew 27:21-23	Mark 15	Luke 23:18-19	John 19:10-12
			have power to release thee?
			11. Jesus answered, Thou couldest have no power at all against me, except it were given thee from above: therefore he that delivered me unto thee hath the greater sin.
			12. And from thenceforth Pilate sought to <u>release</u> him:
21. The governor answered and said unto them, Whether of the twain will ye that I release unto you? They said, Barabbas. 22. Pilate saith unto them, What shall I do then with Jesus which is called Christ? They all say unto him, Let him be crucified. 23. And the governor said, Why, what evil hath he done? But they cried out the more, saying, Let him be crucified.		18. And they cried out all at once, saying, Away with this man, and release unto us Barabbas: 19. (Who for a certain sedition made in the city, and for murder, was cast into prison.)	<u>NOTE</u>: Pilate left the judgment hall, went back to the multitude, and asked them, again, which of the two they wanted to release. The Jews answered Barabbas. Pilate asked what was he to do with Jesus. The Jews said to crucify him (Matthew 27:21-22). Pilate was pleading with the Jews when he asked what Jesus had done wrong (Matthew 27:23 first part). The Jews responded, "Away with this man (Luke 23:18 first part), let him be crucified (Matthew 27:23 last part) and release unto us Barabbas" (Luke 23:18 last part).

Table 7 (continued)

Matthew 27:24	Mark 15:12-15	Luke 23:20-23	John 19:12-13
NOTE: Pilate asked <u>again</u> (or the second time), "What will ye then that I shall do unto him whom ye call the King of the Jews?" (Mark 15:12, Luke 23:20). The Jews cried out again, "Crucify him" (Mark 15:13, Luke 23:21). Pilate asked, "Why, what evil hath he done?" The Jews stubbornly answered, "Crucify him" (Mark 15:14).	12. And Pilate answered and said <u>again</u> unto them, What will ye then that I shall do unto him whom ye call the King of the Jews?	20. Pilate therefore, willing to release Jesus, spake <u>again</u> to them.	
	13. And they cried out <u>again</u>, Crucify him.	21. But they cried, saying, Crucify him, crucify him.	
After Pilate asked the Jews the <u>third time</u>, "Why, what evil hath he done?", he said he found no cause of death in Jesus, so he would therefore chastise, or scourge, him (a <u>second</u> scourging), and <u>let him go</u> (Luke 23:22). The Jews told Pilate if he let this man go, he was not Caesar's friend (John 19:12 last part). When Pilate heard this threat he knew he couldn't win, so he took water and washed his hands before the multitude saying he was innocent of the blood of Jesus Christ (Matthew 27:24, Mark 15:15 first part, Luke 23:23 last part, John 19:13 first part).	14. Then Pilate said unto them, Why, what evil hath he done? And they cried out the more exceedingly, Crucify him.	22. And he said unto them the <u>third time</u>, Why, what evil hath he done? I have found no cause of death in him: I will therefore <u>chastise him</u>, and <u>let him go</u>.	
		23. And they were instant with loud voices, requiring that he might be crucified.	but the Jews cried out, saying, <u>If thou let this man go</u>, thou art not Caesar's friend: whosoever maketh himself a king speaketh against Caesar.
24. When Pilate saw that he could prevail nothing, but that rather a tumult was made, he took water, and <u>washed his hands</u> before the multitude, saying, I am innocent of the blood of this just	15. And so Pilate, willing to content the people,	And the voices of them and of the chief priests prevailed.	13. When Pilate therefore heard that saying,

71

	Table 7 (continued)		
Matthew 27:24-26	Mark 15:15	Luke 23:24-25	John 19:13-16
person: see ye to it. 25. Then answered all the people, and said, <u>His blood be on us</u>, and on our children.			
			he <u>brought Jesus forth</u>, and <u>sat down in the judgment seat</u> in a place that is called the Pavement, but in the Hebrew, Gabbatha.
		24. And Pilate <u>gave sentence</u> that it should be as they required.	
26. Then released he Barabbas unto them:	released Barabbas unto them,	25. And he released unto them him that for sedition and murder was cast into prison, whom they had desired;	
NOTE: After the Jews told Pilate, "His blood be on us, and on our children" (Matthew 27:25), Pilate sentenced Jesus to be crucified. After he released Barabbas, he presented Jesus to the Jews as their king and the chief priests responded, "We have no king but Caesar" (John 19:13-15, Luke 23:24,25 first part, Matthew 27:26 first part, Mark 15:15 middle part).			14. And it was the preparation of the passover, and about the sixth hour: and he saith unto the Jews, Behold your King! 15. But they cried out, Away with him, away with him, crucify him. Pilate saith unto them, Shall I crucify your King? The chief priests answered, We have no king but Caesar.
and when he had <u>scourged Jesus</u>, he delivered him to be crucified.	and delivered Jesus, when he had <u>scourged him</u>, to be crucified.	but he delivered Jesus to their will.	16. Then delivered he him therefore unto them to be crucified.

After Pilate scourged Jesus a <u>second</u> time, he delivered him to be crucified (Matthew 27:26 last part, Mark 15:15 last part, Luke 23:25 last part, John 19:16). The first time Jesus was scourged is recorded in John 19:1 on page 68.

The following explanation of the "sixth hour" in John 19:14 in Table 7 on page 72 is taken from Scofield's Reference Bible. John uses Roman time with the hours starting at 12 midnight and 12 noon, as is done today. However, the Synoptics (Matthew, Mark and Luke) use Hebrew reckoning, beginning with sunrise (i.e. 6 a.m.; 7 a.m. being the first hour). This is apparent from the care with which Matthew, Mark and Luke specify particular hours in relation to the crucifixion. Jesus was put on the cross at 9 a.m. ("third hour" Mark 15:25 page 77); darkness was over the land from noon until 3 p.m. ("sixth" till "ninth hour," Matthew 27:45, Mark 15:33, Luke 23:44 on page 80). Thus in John 19:14 the "sixth hour" could not be Hebrew time (noon), but rather 6 a.m.

Chapter 8

The Crucifixion

After Jesus was scourged the second time, he was stripped, clothed in a scarlet robe, crowned with thorns and mocked. After his own clothes were put back on him, he was led away to be crucified (Matthew 27:27-31, Mark 15:16-20 in Table 8). Jesus carried his cross at first, but then a Cyrenian named Simon was forced to follow Jesus and carry the cross to Golgotha (John 19:17 first part, Matthew 27:32, Mark 15:21, Luke 23:26). Before he was crucified, Jesus refused a mixture of fluids that would have dulled the pain (Matthew 27:34, Mark 15:23). A placard was placed above Jesus' head on the cross; the Gospel of John describes the <u>placing</u> of the placard on the cross <u>during</u> the crucifixion while Matthew, Mark and Luke describe <u>seeing</u> the title <u>after</u> Jesus was crucified (John 19:19-22, Matthew 27:37, Mark 15:26, Luke 23:38).

Table 8			
Matthew 27:27-29	Mark 15:16-18	Luke 23	John 19
27. Then the soldiers of the governor took Jesus into the common hall, and gathered unto him the whole band of soldiers.	16. And the soldiers led him away into the hall, called Praetorium; and they call together the whole band.		
28. And they stripped him, and put on him a <u>scarlet</u> robe.			
	17. And they clothed him with purple,		
29. And when they had plaited a crown of thorns, they put it upon his head, and a reed in his right hand: and they bowed the knee before him, and mocked him, saying, Hail, King of the Jews!	and plaited a crown of thorns, and put it about his head, 18. And began to salute him, Hail, King of the Jews!		

Table 8 (continued)

Matthew 27:30-32	Mark 15:19-21	Luke 23:26-28	John 19:16-17
30. And they spit upon him, and took the reed, and smote him on the head.	19. And they smote him on the head with a reed, and did spit upon him, and bowing their knees worshipped him.		
31. And after that they had mocked him, they took the robe off from him, and put his own raiment on him,	20. And when they had mocked him, they took off the purple from him, and put his own clothes on him,		
and led him away to crucify him.	and led him out to crucify him.		And they took Jesus, and led him away. 17. And he bearing his cross went forth
32. And as they came out, they found a man of Cyrene, Simon by name: him they compelled to bear his cross.	21. And they compel one Simon a Cyrenian, who passed by, coming out of the country, the father of Alexander and Rufus, to bear his cross.	26. And as they led him away, they laid hold upon one Simon, a Cyrenian, coming out of the country, and on him they laid the cross, that he might bear it after Jesus.	
		27. And there followed him a great company of people, and of women, which also bewailed and lamented him. 28. But Jesus turning unto them said, Daughters of Jerusalem, weep not for me, but weep for yourselves, and for your children.	

75

Table 8 (continued)

Matthew 27:33-35	Mark 15:22-23	Luke 23:29-34	John 19:17-20
		29. For, behold, the days are coming, in the which they shall say, Blessed are the barren, and the wombs that never bare, and the paps which never gave suck. 30. Then shall they begin to say to the mountains, Fall on us; and to the hills, Cover us. 31. For if they do these things in a green tree, what shall be done in the dry? 32. And there were also two other, malefactors, led with him to be put to death.	
33. And when they were come unto a place called Golgotha, that is to say, a place of a skull, 34. They gave him vinegar to drink mingled with gall: and when he had tasted thereof, he would not drink.	22. And they bring him unto the place Golgotha, which is, being interpreted, The place of a skull. 23. And they gave him to drink wine mingled with myrrh: but he received it not.	33. And when they were come to the place, which is called Calvary,	into a place called the place of a skull, which is called in the Hebrew Golgotha:
35. And they crucified him,		there they crucified him, and the malefactors, one on the right hand, and the other on the left.	18. Where they crucified him, and two other with him, on either side one, and Jesus in the midst.
		34. Then said Jesus, Father, forgive them; for they know not what they do.	19. And Pilate wrote a title, and put it on the cross. And the writing was, JESUS OF NAZARETH THE KING OF THE JEWS. 20. This title then read many of the Jews: for the place where

Table 8 (continued)

Matthew 27:35-36	Mark 15:24-25	Luke 23:34-35	John 19:20-24
			Jesus was crucified was nigh to the city: and it was written in Hebrew, and Greek, and Latin. 21. Then said the chief priests of the Jews to Pilate, Write not, The King of the Jews; but that he said, I am King of the Jews. 22. Pilate answered, What I have written I have written.
	24. And when they had crucified him,		23. Then the soldiers, when they had crucified Jesus, took his garments, and <u>made four parts</u>, to every soldier a part; and also his coat: now the coat was without seam, woven from the top throughout.
and parted his garments,	they parted his garments,	And they parted his raiment,	24. They said therefore among themselves, Let us not rend it, but <u>cast lots</u> for it, whose it shall be:
<u>casting lots</u>:	<u>casting lots</u> upon them, what every man should take.	and <u>cast lots</u>.	
that it might be fulfilled which was spoken by the prophet, They parted my garments among them, and upon my vesture did they cast lots.			that the scripture might be fulfilled, which saith, They parted my raiment among them, and for my vesture they did cast lots. These things therefore the soldiers did.
	25. And it was the third hour, and (or <u>when</u>) they crucified him.		**NOTE**: Mark 15:25 is discussed further on page 78.
36. And sitting down they watched him there;		35. And the people stood beholding. And the rulers also	

Table 8 (continued)			
Matthew 27:37-38	Mark 15:26-28	Luke 23:35-38	John 19
37. And set up over his head his accusation written, THIS IS JESUS THE KING OF THE JEWS.	26. And the superscription of his accusation was written over, THE KING OF THE JEWS.	with them derided him, saying, He saved others; let him save himself, if he be Christ, the chosen of God. 36. And the soldiers also mocked him, coming to him, and offering him vinegar, 37. And saying, If thou be the king of the Jews, save thyself. 38. And a superscription also was written over him in letters of Greek, and Latin, and Hebrew, THIS IS THE KING OF THE JEWS.	
38. Then (or at the time) were there two thieves crucified with him, one on the right hand, and another on the left.	27. And with him they crucify two thieves; the one on his right hand, and the other on his left.		**NOTE**: The word "Then" in Matthew 27:38 can also be translated "at the time" (Strong's Concordance, Greek Dictionary, word #5119).
	28. And the scripture was fulfilled, which saith, And he was numbered with the transgressors.		

Mark 15:25 on page 77 tells us the time <u>when</u> Jesus was crucified (9 a.m.). The word translated "<u>and</u>" in verse 25 can be translated "<u>when</u>" (Strong's Concordance, Greek Dictionary, word #2532). Mark 15:25 in the New International and Revised Standard Versions of the Bible is shown below.

Mark 15:25 (New International Version)
25. It was the third hour <u>when</u> they crucified him.

Mark 15:25 (Revised Standard Version)
25. And it was the third hour, <u>when</u> they crucified him.

Also, for more information on the times of the various events associated with the crucifixion, see the information on page 73.

Chapter 9

Jesus Dies

As Jesus hung on the cross and was derided and mocked, one of the two thieves crucified with him said, "If thou be Christ, save thyself and us." The other thief asked Jesus to remember him when he came into his kingdom. Jesus told the second thief he would be with him in paradise (Matthew 27:39-44, Mark 15:29-32, Luke 23:39-43 in Table 9).

Table 9			
Matthew 27:39-43	Mark 15:29-32	Luke 23	John 19
39. And they that passed by reviled him, wagging their heads, 40. And saying, Thou that destroyest the temple, and buildest it in three days, save thyself. If thou be the Son of God, come down from the cross. 41. Likewise also the chief priests mocking him, with the scribes and elders, said, 42. He saved others; himself he cannot save. If he be the King of Israel, let him now come down from the cross, and we will believe him. 43. He trusted in God; let him deliver him	29. And they that passed by railed on him, wagging their heads, and saying, Ah, thou that destroyest the temple, and buildest it in three days, 30. Save thyself, and come down from the cross. 31. Likewise also the chief priests mocking said among themselves with the scribes, He saved others; himself he cannot save. 32. Let Christ the King of Israel descend now from the cross, that we may see and believe.		

79

Table 9 (continued)			
Matthew 27:43-46	Mark 15:32-34	Luke 23:39-45	John 19
now, if he will have him: for he said, I am the Son of God.			
44. The thieves also, which were crucified with him, cast the same in his teeth.	And they that were crucified with him reviled him.		
		39. And one of the malefactors which were hanged railed on him, saying, If thou be Christ, save thyself and us. 40. But the other answering rebuked him, saying, Dost not thou fear God, seeing thou art in the same condemnation? 41. And we indeed justly; for we receive the due reward of our deeds: but this man hath done nothing amiss. 42. And he said unto Jesus, Lord, remember me when thou comest into thy kingdom. 43. And Jesus said unto him, Verily I say unto thee, To day shalt thou be with me in paradise.	
45. Now from the sixth hour there was darkness over all the land unto the ninth hour. 46. And about the ninth hour Jesus cried with a loud voice, saying, Eli, Eli, lama sabachthani? that is to say, My God, my God, why hast thou forsaken me?	33. And when the sixth hour was come, there was darkness over the whole land until the ninth hour. 34. And at the ninth hour Jesus cried with a loud voice, saying, Eloi, Eloi, lama sabachthani? which is, being interpreted, My God, my God, why hast thou forsaken me?	44. And it was about the sixth hour, and there was a darkness over all the earth until the ninth hour. 45. And the sun was darkened,	**NOTE**: From the sixth hour to the ninth hour (12 noon to 3 p.m.), it was dark (Matthew 27:45, Mark 15:33, Luke 23:44). At 3 p.m. it got even darker and Jesus cried with a loud voice, "My God, my God, why hast thou forsaken me?" (Matthew 27:46, Mark 15:34, Luke 23:45 first part).

Table 9 (continued)			
Matthew 27:47-49	Mark 15:35-36	Luke 23	John 19:25-29
47. Some of them that stood there, when they heard that, said, This man calleth for Elias.	35. And some of them that stood by, when they heard it, said, Behold, he calleth Elias.		
NOTE: After Jesus gave John the responsibility of taking care of his mother, he said he was thirsty (John 19:25-28). The other Jews wouldn't allow it, so Jesus' own disciples gave him vinegar to drink (Matthew 27:48-49, Mark 15:36, John 19:29 pages 81-82). When Jesus received the vinegar, he said, "It is finished," and the top of the veil was torn in the middle (John 19:30 first part, Luke 23:45 last part). After Jesus cried with a loud voice, he said, "Father, into thy hands I commend my spirit" (Mark 15:37 first part, Luke 23:46 first part). After Jesus cried aloud _again_, he bowed his head and died (Matthew 27:50, Mark 15:37 last part, Luke 23:46 last part, John 19:30 middle and last parts).			25. Now there stood by the cross of Jesus his mother, and his mother's sister, Mary the wife of Cleophas, and Mary Magdalene. 26. When Jesus therefore saw his mother, and the disciple standing by, whom he loved, he saith unto his mother, Woman, behold thy son! 27. Then saith he to the disciple, Behold thy mother! And from that hour that disciple took her unto his own home. 28. After this, Jesus knowing that all things were now accomplished, that the scripture might be fulfilled, saith, I thirst. 29. Now there was set a vessel full of vinegar:
48. And straightway one of them ran, and took a sponge, and filled it with vinegar, and put it on a reed, and gave him to drink.	36. And one ran and filled a sponge full of vinegar, and put it on a reed, and gave him to drink,		
49. The rest said, _Let be_ (or _wait_), let us see whether Elias will come to save him.	saying, _Let alone_ (or _wait_); let us see whether Elias will come to take him down.		

Table 9 (continued)			
Matthew 27:50-51	Mark 15:37-38	Luke 23:45-46	John 19:29-30
			and they filled a sponge with vinegar, and put it upon hyssop, and put it to his mouth. 30. When Jesus therefore had received the vinegar, he said, It is finished:
		and the veil of the temple was rent in the midst.	
	37. And Jesus cried with a loud voice,		
		46. And when Jesus had cried with a loud voice, he said, Father, into thy hands I commend my spirit: and having said thus,	**NOTE**: Jesus cried with a loud voice <u>twice</u> before he died. The first time is recorded in Mark 15:37 first part. The second time is recorded in Matthew 27:50 first part.
50. Jesus, when he had cried <u>again</u> with a loud voice,			and he bowed his head,
yielded up the ghost. 51. And, behold, the veil of the temple was rent in twain from the top to the bottom;	and gave up the ghost. 38. And the veil of the temple was rent in twain from the top to the bottom.	he gave up the ghost.	and gave up the ghost.

The rending or tearing of the veil <u>began</u> at the top in the middle of the veil when Jesus said, "It is finished" (John 19:30 first part and Luke 23:45 last part), and <u>ended</u> at the bottom of the veil right after he died (Matthew 27:51, Mark 15:38).

Chapter 10

Jesus' Burial

After the veil was torn, the earth quaked, graves were opened and the centurion and those with him said, "Truly this was the Son of God" (Matthew 27:51-54, Mark 15:39, Luke 23:47 in Table 10-1). As the disciples watched, the soldiers broke the legs of the two thieves to hasten their deaths, but did not break Jesus' legs because he was already dead (John 19:31-37, Matthew 27:55-56, Mark 15:40-41, Luke 23:48-49). As evening approached, Joseph of Arimathaea and Nicodemus took Jesus' body, wrapped it in linen with spices and placed it in a tomb. They placed a stone at the door of the tomb and departed (Matthew 27:57-60, Mark 15:42-46, Luke 23:50-54, John 19:38-42).

Table 10-1			
Matthew 27:51-54	Mark 15:39	Luke 23:47	John 19
	39. And when the centurion, which stood over against him, saw that he so cried out, and gave up the ghost, he said, Truly this man was the Son of God.		
and the earth did quake, and the rocks rent; 52. And the graves were opened; and many bodies of the saints which slept arose, 53. And came out of the graves after his resurrection, and went into the holy city, and appeared unto many. 54. Now when the centurion, and they that were with him, watching Jesus, <u>saw</u> the earthquake, and those things that were done, they feared greatly, saying, Truly this was the Son of God.		47. Now when the centurion saw what was done, he glorified God, saying, Certainly this was a righteous man.	

83

Table 10-1 (continued)			
Matthew 27:55-56	Mark 15:40-41	Luke 23:48-49	John 19:31-35
			31. The Jews therefore, because it was the preparation, that the bodies should not remain upon the cross on the sabbath day, (for that sabbath day was an high day,) besought Pilate that their legs might be broken, and that they might be taken away. 32. Then came the soldiers, and brake the legs of the first, and of the other which was crucified with him. 33. But when they came to Jesus, and saw that he was dead already, they brake not his legs: 34. But one of the soldiers with a spear pierced his side, and forthwith came there out blood and water.
		48. And all the people that came together to that sight, beholding the things which were done, smote their breasts, and returned.	
55. And many <u>women</u> were there beholding afar off, which followed Jesus from Galilee, ministering unto him: 56. Among which was Mary Magdalene, and Mary the mother of James and Joses, and the	40. There were also <u>women</u> looking on afar off: among whom was Mary Magdalene, and Mary the mother of James the less and of Joses, and Salome; 41. (Who also, when he was in Galilee, followed him, and	49. And all <u>his</u> <u>acquaintance</u>, and the <u>women</u> that followed him from Galilee, stood afar off, <u>beholding</u> these things.	35. And <u>he</u> that <u>saw</u> it bare record, and his record is true: and he knoweth that he saith true, that ye might believe.

Table 10-1 (continued)			
Matthew 27:56-58	Mark 15:41-45	Luke 23:50-52	John 19:36-38
mother of Zebedee's children.	ministered unto him;) and many other women which came up with him unto Jerusalem.		
			36. For these things were done, that the scripture should be fulfilled, A bone of him shall not be broken. 37. And again another scripture saith, They shall look on him whom they pierced.
57. When the even was come, there came a rich man of Arimathaea, named Joseph, who also himself was Jesus' disciple: 58. He went to Pilate, and begged the body of Jesus.	42. And now when the even was come, because it was the preparation, that is, the day before the sabbath, 43. Joseph of Arimathaea, an honourable counsellor, which also waited for the kingdom of God, came, and went in boldly unto Pilate, and craved the body of Jesus. 44. And Pilate marvelled if he were already dead: and calling unto him the centurion, he asked him whether he had been any while dead. 45. And when he knew it of the centurion,	50. And, behold, there was a man named Joseph, a counsellor; and he was a good man, and a just: 51. (The same had not consented to the counsel and deed of them;) he was of Arimathaea, a city of the Jews: who also himself waited for the kingdom of God. 52. This man went unto Pilate, and begged the body of Jesus.	38. And after this Joseph of Arimathaea, being a disciple of Jesus, but secretly for fear of the Jews, besought Pilate that he might take away the body of Jesus:

Table 10-1 (continued)			
Matthew 27:58-60	Mark 15:45-46	Luke 23:53-54	John 19:38-42
Then Pilate commanded the body to be delivered.	he gave the body to Joseph.		and Pilate gave him leave.
59. And when Joseph had taken the body,	46. And he bought fine linen, and took him down,	53. And he took it down,	He came therefore, and took the body of Jesus.
			39. And there came also Nicodemus, which at the first came to Jesus by night, and brought a mixture of myrrh and aloes, about an hundred pound weight.
he wrapped it in a clean linen cloth,	and wrapped him in the linen,	and wrapped it in linen,	40. Then took they the body of Jesus, and wound it in linen clothes with the spices, as the manner of the Jews is to bury.
			41. Now in the place where he was crucified there was a garden; and in the garden a new sepulchre, wherein was never man yet laid.
60. And laid it in his own new tomb, which he had hewn out in the rock:	and laid him in a sepulchre which was hewn out of a rock,	and laid it in a sepulchre that was hewn in stone, wherein never man before was laid.	42. There laid they Jesus therefore
and he rolled a great stone to the door of the sepulchre, and departed.	and rolled a stone unto the door of the sepulchre.		
		54. And that day was the preparation, and the sabbath drew on.	because of the Jews' preparation day; for the sepulchre was nigh at hand.

Jesus Christ is our passover and he died and was buried in the late afternoon of the day God calls the passover.

I Corinthians 5:7

7. Purge out therefore the old leaven, that ye may be a new lump, as ye are unleavened. For even Christ our passover is sacrificed for us:

I Peter 1:18-19

18. Forasmuch as ye know that ye were not redeemed with corruptible things, as silver and gold, from your vain conversation received by tradition from your fathers;
19. But with the precious blood of Christ, as of <u>a lamb without blemish and without spot</u>:

Exodus 12:1-3,5-8,11

1. AND the Lord spake unto Moses and Aaron in the land of Egypt, saying,
2. This month shall be unto you the beginning of months: it shall be the first month of the year to you.
3. Speak ye unto all the congregation of Israel, saying, In the tenth day of this month they shall take to them every man a lamb, according to the house of their fathers, a lamb for an house:
5. Your <u>lamb shall be without blemish</u>, a male of the first year: ye shall take it out from the sheep, or from the goats:
6. And ye shall keep it up until the fourteenth day of the same month: and the whole assembly of the congregation of Israel shall kill it in the evening.
7. And they shall take of the blood, and strike it on the two side posts and on the upper door post of the houses, wherein they shall eat it.
8. And they shall eat the flesh in that night, roast with fire, and unleavened bread; and with bitter herbs they shall eat it.
11. And thus shall ye eat it; with your loins girded, your shoes on your feet, and your staff in your hand; and ye shall eat it in haste: it is the Lord's <u>passover</u>.

The meal described in Exodus 12 above is the same meal Jesus and his disciples ate in the goodman's house (Luke 22:15 page 13). The passover day is a preparation day (John 19:14 page 72). A <u>preparation day</u> is a day which <u>comes before a sabbath</u> (Mark 15:42 page 85). Leviticus 23:4-7 shows that the sabbath (or holy day) which <u>follows</u> the <u>passover day</u> is the first day of the seven days of unleavened bread. The first day of unleavened bread is a sabbath that occurs only <u>once a year</u> (hence a "high day" in John 19:31 page 84). This "annual or yearly" sabbath does not necessarily occur on the same day of the week as the weekly sabbath. Leviticus 23:32 and Genesis 1:5-6,8 show that all sabbaths are observed from sunset to sunset and, in the Bible, each day begins and ends at sunset, not at midnight.

Leviticus 23:4-7

4. These are the feasts of the LORD, even holy convocations, which ye shall proclaim in their seasons.
5. In the <u>fourteenth day</u> of the first month at even is the LORD'S <u>passover</u>.
6. And on the <u>fifteenth day</u> of the <u>same month</u> is the <u>feast of unleavened bread</u> unto the LORD: <u>seven days</u> ye must eat unleavened bread.
7. In the <u>first day</u> ye shall have an <u>holy convocation</u>: ye shall do no servile work therein.

Leviticus 23:32

32. It shall be unto you a sabbath of rest, and ye shall afflict your souls: in the ninth day of the month at even, **from even unto even,** shall ye **celebrate your sabbath.**

Genesis 1:5-6,8

5. And God called the light Day, and the darkness he called Night. And <u>the evening and the morning were the first day</u>.
6. And God said, Let there be a firmament in the midst of the waters . . .
8. And God called the firmament Heaven. And <u>the evening and the morning were the second day</u> (see also Genesis 1:13,19,23,31 in which the day begins at evening).

So Jesus died and was buried on a preparation day and, as will be seen shortly, the sabbath that followed this preparation day did not occur on the same day of the week as the weekly sabbath.

Now continuing in Table 10-2, as Jesus' body was carried to the tomb, Mary Magdalene and the other Mary followed. After they beheld the tomb and how Jesus' body was laid, they left (Matthew 27:61, Mark 15:47, Luke 23:55-56). On the day that followed the passover, or on the first day of unleavened bread, the chief priests and Pharisees asked Pilate to set a guard at the tomb to prevent Jesus' disciples from stealing his body and saying he was risen from the dead (Matthew 27:62-66). On the day that followed the first day of unleavened bread, Mary Magdalene and the other women bought and prepared sweet spices to anoint Jesus' body (Mark 16:1 and Luke 23:56 page 89). After the women bought and prepared the spices, they rested on the weekly sabbath day according to the commandment in Exodus 20:8-11 and Deuteronomy 5:12-15 (Luke 23:56 last part). Then early on Sunday morning the women brought the spices to the tomb to anoint Jesus' body (Matthew 28:1, Mark 16:2, Luke 24:1, John 20:1).

Table 10-2			
Matthew 27:61-65	Mark 15:47	Luke 23:55-56	John 19
61. And there was Mary Magdalene, and the other Mary, sitting over against the sepulchre.	47. And Mary Magdalene and Mary the mother of Joses beheld where he was laid.	55. And the women also, which came with him from Galilee, followed after, and beheld the sepulchre, and how his body was laid. 56. And they returned,	
62. Now the next day, that followed the day of the preparation, the chief priests and Pharisees came together unto Pilate, 63. Saying, Sir, we remember that that deceiver said, while he was yet alive, After three days I will rise again. 64. Command therefore that the sepulchre be made sure until the third day, lest his disciples come by night, and steal him away, and say unto the people, He is risen from the dead: so the last error shall be worse than the first. 65. Pilate said unto them, Ye have a watch: go your			

Table 10-3				
Day of the Week	Matt 27:60-63	Mark 15:46-47	Luke 23:53-56	John 19:42
On Wednesday afternoon shortly before sunset	60. And laid it in his own new tomb, which he had hewn out in the rock:	46. . . . and laid him in a sepulchre which was hewn out of a rock,	53. . . . and laid it in a sepulchre that was hewn in stone, wherein never man before was laid.	42. There laid they Jesus therefore
	and he rolled a great stone to the door of the sepulchre, and departed.	and rolled a stone unto the door of the sepulchre.		
			54. And that day was the **preparation,** and **the sabbath drew on**.	because of the Jews' preparation day; for the sepulchre was nigh at hand.
	61. And there was Mary Magdalene, and the other Mary, sitting over against the sepulchre.	47. And Mary Magdalene and Mary the mother of Joses beheld where he was laid.	55. And the women also, which came with him from Galilee, followed after, and beheld the sepulchre, and how his body was laid.	
			56. And they returned,	
Between Wednesday sunset and Thursday sunset (the first day of unleavened bread)	62. Now **the next day, that followed the day of the preparation** (the first day of unleavened bread), the chief priests and Pharisees came together unto Pilate,			
	63. Saying, Sir, we remember that that deceiver said, while he was yet alive, After three days I will rise again.			

Day of the Week	Matt 27:64-66	Mark 16:1	Luke 23:56	John 19
Between Wednesday sunset and Thursday sunset (the first day of unleavened bread)	64. Command therefore that the sepulchre be made sure until the third day, lest his disciples come by night, and steal him away, and say unto the people, He is risen from the dead: so the last error shall be worse than the first. 65. Pilate said unto them, Ye have a watch: go your way, make it as sure as ye can. 66. So they went, and made the sepulchre sure, sealing the stone, and setting a watch.			
Between Thursday sunset and Friday sunset		1. AND **when the sabbath** (the first day of unleavened bread) **was past**, Mary Magdalene, and Mary the mother of James, and Salome, had **bought** sweet spices, that they might come and anoint him.	and **prepared spices and ointments;**	

Table 10-3 (continued)

Table 10-3 (continued)				
Day of the Week	Matt 28:1	Mark 16:2	Luke 23:56;24:1	John 20:1
Between Friday sunset and Saturday sunset (weekly sabbath)			and **rested** the **sabbath day** (weekly sabbath day) according to the commandment.	
On Sunday morning at dawn (between Saturday sunset and Sunday sunset)	1. IN the end of the sabbath, as it began to dawn toward the first day of the week, came Mary Magdalene and the other Mary to see the sepulchre.	2. And very early in the morning the first day of the week, they came unto the sepulchre at the rising of the sun.	1. NOW **upon the first day of the week**, very early in the morning, they came unto the sepulchre, **bringing** the spices which they had prepared, and certain others with them.	1. THE first day of the week cometh Mary Magdalene early, when it was yet dark, unto the sepulchre,

Jesus Christ died and was buried on a Wednesday afternoon, shortly before sunset. God the Father resurrected him late in the afternoon on Saturday, exactly three days and three nights after his body was placed in the tomb. By the time the women arrived at the tomb on Sunday morning, Jesus Christ was already risen. He had been resurrected and had been alive again for approximately twelve hours!

Chapter 11

He Is Risen

As the women approached the tomb, a great earthquake occurred as an angel descended from heaven and rolled back the stone from the door of the tomb and sat on it (Matthew 28:2-4, Mark 16:3-4, Luke 24:2, John 20:1 in Table 11).

Table 11			
Matthew 28:2-6	Mark 16:3-4	Luke 24:2	John 20:1
2. And, behold, there was a great earthquake: for the angel of the Lord descended from heaven, and came and rolled back the stone from the door, and sat upon it. 3. His countenance was like lightning, and his raiment white as snow: 4. And for fear of him the keepers did shake, and became as dead men. 5. And the angel answered and said unto the women, Fear not ye: for I know that ye seek Jesus, which was crucified. 6. He is not here: for he is risen, as he	3. And they said among themselves, Who shall roll us away the stone from the door of the sepulchre? 4. And when they looked, they saw that the stone was rolled away: for it was very great.	2. And they found the stone rolled away from the sepulchre.	and seeth the stone taken away from the sepulchre.

Table 11 (continued)			
Matthew 28:6-7	Mark 16:5-7	Luke 24:3-6	John 20
said. <u>Come, see the place where the Lord lay</u>. 7. And go quickly, and tell his disciples that he is risen from the dead; and, behold, he goeth before you into Galilee; there shall ye see him: lo, I have told you.	5. And <u>entering into the sepulchre</u>, they saw a young man sitting on the right side, clothed in a long white garment; and they were affrighted. 6. And he saith unto them, Be not affrighted: Ye seek Jesus of Nazareth, which was crucified: he is risen; <u>he is not here</u> behold the place where they laid him. 7. But go your way, tell his disciples and Peter that he goeth before you into Galilee: there shall ye see him, as he said unto you.	3. And <u>they entered in</u>, and <u>found not the body</u> of the Lord Jesus. 4. And it came to pass, as they were <u>much perplexed</u> thereabout, behold, two men stood by them in shining garments: 5. And as they were afraid, and bowed down their faces to the earth, they said unto them, Why seek ye the living among the dead? 6. He is not here, but is risen: remember how he spake unto you when he was yet	<u>NOTES</u>: 1) In Matthew 28:5-7 the angel told the women Jesus was not at the tomb, but was risen, and after they saw the place where Jesus lay they were to tell his disciples he was risen from the dead and would meet them in Galilee. 2) The women did not comprehend what the first angel said, so they entered the tomb <u>still looking for Jesus' body</u>. Instead they found a young man (another angel) who told them the same things the first angel did (Mark 16:5-7, Luke 24:3). 3) As the women stood in the tomb much perplexed, or <u>still wondering what had happened to Jesus' body</u>, two angels appeared and asked them why they were looking for the living among the dead. After the angels reminded them of what Jesus had said in Galilee, the women <u>remembered</u> and left the tomb to tell the disciples (Luke 24:4-9, Matthew 28:8, Mark 16:8 and John 20:2 first part).

Table 11 (continued)			
Matthew 28:8	Mark 16:8	Luke 24:6-12	John 20:2-5
		in Galilee, 7. Saying, The Son of man must be delivered into the hands of sinful men, and be crucified, and the third day rise again. 8. And <u>they remembered his words</u>,	
8. And they departed quickly from the sepulchre with fear and great joy; and did <u>run</u> to bring his disciples word. **NOTE**: With the women on foot and the disciples in their own homes (John 20:10 page 97), it took time for the women to tell the disciples what they had seen. Initially the disciples did not believe the women (Luke 24:9-11). But after Mary Magdalene told Peter and John (John 20:2 last part) and Peter and John ran to the tomb and looked inside, John believed. Peter and John returned to their homes, but Mary Magdalene stayed at the tomb (John 20:3-11, Luke 24:12).	8. And they went out quickly, and <u>fled from the sepulchre</u>; for they trembled and were amazed: neither said they any thing to any man; for they were afraid.	9. And <u>returned from the sepulchre</u>, and told all these things unto the eleven, and to all the rest. 10. It was Mary Magdalene, and Joanna, and Mary the mother of James, and other women that were with them, which told these things unto the apostles. 11. And their words seemed to them as idle tales, and they believed them not. 12. Then arose Peter, and ran unto the sepulchre;	2. Then she (Mary Magdalene) <u>runneth</u>, and cometh to Simon Peter, and to the other disciple, whom Jesus loved, and saith unto them, They have taken away the Lord out of the sepulchre, and we know not where they have laid him. 3. Peter therefore went forth, and that other disciple, and came to the sepulchre. 4. So they ran both together: and the other disciple did outrun Peter, and came first to the sepulchre. 5. And he stooping down, and looking in, saw the linen

			Table 11 (continued)
Matthew 28	Mark 16	Luke 24:12	John 20:5-13
			clothes lying; yet went he not in.
			6. Then cometh Simon Peter following him,
		and stooping down,	and went into the sepulchre,
		he beheld the linen clothes laid by themselves,	and seeth the linen clothes lie,
			7. And the napkin, that was about his head, not lying with the linen clothes, but wrapped together in a place by itself.
			8. Then went in also that other disciple, which came first to the sepulchre, and he saw, and believed.
			9. For as yet they knew not the scripture, that he must rise again from the dead.
		and departed, wondering in himself at that which was come to pass.	10. Then the disciples went away again unto their own home.
			11. But Mary stood without at the sepulchre weeping: and as she wept, she stooped down, and looked into the sepulchre,
			12. And seeth two angels in white sitting, the one at the head, and the other at the feet, where the body of Jesus had lain.
			13. And they say unto her, Woman, why weepest thou? She saith unto them,

Table 11 (continued)			
Matthew 28:9-10	Mark 16:9-11	Luke 24	John 20:13-18
NOTES: 1) Jesus appeared to Mary Magdalene at the tomb where he told her to <u>not touch</u> him because he had not yet ascended to his Father (John 20:14-17, Mark 16:9). After he returned to earth from heaven, he appeared to the other women who were still telling the disciples what they had seen <u>at the tomb</u>. He allowed these women to <u>hold him</u> by the feet (Matthew 28:9). 2) Mary went and told the disciples she had <u>seen Jesus</u>, but they didn't believe her (John 20:18, Mark 16:10-11). With the distances Mary and the other women had to walk, its certainly possible that Jesus met the other women during the same period of time Mary was telling the disciples she had seen Jesus (Matthew 28:9).	9. Now when Jesus was risen early the first day of the week, <u>he appeared first to Mary Magdalene</u>, out of whom he had cast seven devils.		Because they have taken away my Lord, and I know not where they have laid him. 14. And when she had thus said, she turned herself back, and <u>saw Jesus standing</u>, and knew not that it was Jesus. 15. Jesus saith unto her, Woman, why weepest thou? whom seekest thou? She, supposing him to be the gardener, saith unto him, Sir, if thou have borne him hence, tell me where thou hast laid him, and I will take him away. 16. Jesus saith unto her, Mary. She turned herself, and saith unto him, Rabboni; which is to say, Master. 17. Jesus saith unto her, <u>Touch me not</u>; for I am not yet ascended to my Father: but go to my brethren, and say unto them, I ascend unto my Father, and your Father; and to my God, and your God.
9. And as they went to tell his disciples, behold, Jesus met them, saying, All hail. And they came and <u>held him</u> by the feet, and worshipped him. 10. Then said Jesus unto them, Be not afraid: go tell my	10. And she went and told them that had been with him, as they mourned and wept. 11. And they, when they had heard that he was alive, and had been seen of her, believed not.		18. Mary Magdalene came and told the disciples that she had seen the Lord, and that he had spoken these things unto her.

Table 11 (continued)			
Matthew 28:10-15	Mark 16:12	Luke 24:13-19	John 20
brethren that they go into Galilee, and there shall they see me.			
11. Now when they were going, behold, some of the watch came into the city, and shewed unto the chief priests all the things that were done. 12. And when they were assembled with the elders, and had taken counsel, they gave large money unto the soldiers, 13. Saying, Say ye, His disciples came by night, and stole him away while we slept. 14. And if this come to the governor's ears, we will persuade him, and secure you. 15. So they took the money, and did as they were taught: and this saying is commonly reported among the Jews until this day.	12. After that <u>he appeared</u> in another <u>form</u> unto <u>two of them</u>, as they walked, and went into the country.	13. And, behold, <u>two of them</u> went that same day to a village called Emmaus, which was from Jerusalem about threescore furlongs. 14. And they talked together of all these things which had happened. 15. And it came to pass, that, while they communed together and reasoned, <u>Jesus himself drew near</u>, and went with them. 16. But <u>their eyes were holden</u> that they should not know him. 17. And he said unto them, What manner of communications are these that ye have one to another, as ye walk, and are sad? 18. And the one of them, whose name was Cleopas, answering said unto him, Art thou only a stranger in Jerusalem, and hast not known the things which are come to pass there in these days? 19. And he said unto them, What things? And they said unto him, Concerning Jesus of Nazareth, which was a prophet mighty in deed and word before God and all the people:	**NOTES**: While the women were telling the disciples to meet Jesus in Galilee: 1) Some of those on watch at the tomb came and told the chief priests what had happened (Matthew 28:11-15) and 2) Jesus appeared in another form to two disciples as they walked into the country (Luke 24: 13-32, Mark 16:12).

Table 11 (continued)			
Matthew 28	Mark 16	Luke 24:20-27	John 20
		20. And how the chief priests and our rulers delivered him to be condemned to death, and have crucified him.	
		21. But we trusted that it had been he which should have redeemed Israel: and beside all this, to day is the third day since these things were done.	
		22. Yea, and certain women also of our company made us astonished, which were early at the sepulchre;	
		23. And when they found not his body, they came, saying, that they had also seen a vision of angels, which said that he was alive.	
		24. And certain of them which were with us went to the sepulchre, and found it even so as the women had said: but him they saw not.	
		25. Then he said unto them, O fools, and slow of heart to believe all that the prophets have spoken:	
		26. Ought not Christ to have suffered these things, and to enter into his glory.	
		27. And beginning at Moses and all the prophets, he expounded unto them in all the scriptures the things concerning himself.	

Table 11 (continued)			
Matthew 28	Mark 16:13	Luke 24:28-35	John 20
NOTE: <u>On Sunday afternoon</u>, after Jesus disappeared before their eyes at supper, the two disciples returned to Jerusalem and told the eleven apostles what had happened, but they did not believe them (Luke 24:31,33-35, Mark 16:13). Thomas was one of the original twelve apostles (Matthew 10:1-4, Mark 3:13-19, Luke 6:13-16) and Judas Iscariot was dead, so Thomas <u>had to be present</u> for the "<u>eleven</u>" to be together (Luke 24:33 last part).	13. And <u>they went</u> and <u>told it</u> unto the residue: neither believed they them.	28. And they drew nigh unto the village, whither they went: and he made as though he would have gone further. 29. But they constrained him, saying, Abide with us: for it is toward evening, and the day is far spent. And he went in to tarry with them. 30. And it came to pass, as he sat at meat with them, he took bread, and blessed it, and brake, and gave to them. 31. And their eyes were opened, and they knew him; and he <u>vanished out of their sight</u>. 32. And they said one to another, Did not our heart burn within us, while he talked with us by the way, and while he opened to us the scriptures? 33. And they rose up <u>the same hour</u>, and <u>returned to Jerusalem</u>, and found the <u>eleven</u> gathered together, and them that were with them, 34. Saying, The Lord is risen indeed, and hath appeared to Simon. 35. And they <u>told</u> what things were done in the way, and how he was known of them in breaking of bread.	

Table 11 (continued)			
Matthew 28	Mark 16	Luke 24	John 20:19-25
NOTES: Based on the gospel accounts, Jesus appeared to the apostles, <u>as a group</u>, four times after his resurrection. 1) Thomas was present on Sunday afternoon when the two disciples told the "eleven" they had seen Jesus (see the NOTE on page 101). But when Jesus appeared to the apostles on this <u>same Sunday afternoon</u>, Thomas was <u>not</u> present (John 20:19-24). So, Thomas must have left the other apostles just <u>before</u> Jesus appeared. 2) Like his first appearance, Jesus' second appearance occurred in Jerusalem and is described in the NOTE on page 103. 3) Jesus' third appearance took place in Galilee and is described in the NOTE on page 106. 4) His fourth appearance took place in Galilee and is described in the NOTE on page 110.			19. Then the <u>same day at evening</u>, being the first day of the week, when the doors were shut where the disciples were assembled for fear of the Jews, <u>came Jesus</u> and stood in the midst, and saith unto them, Peace be unto you. 20. And when he had so said, he shewed unto them his hands and his side. Then were the disciples glad, when they saw the Lord. 21. Then said Jesus to them <u>again</u>, Peace be unto you: as my Father hath sent me, even so send I you. 22. And when he had said this, he breathed on them, and saith unto them, Receive ye the Holy Ghost: 23. Whose soever sins ye remit, they are remitted unto them; and whose soever sins ye retain, they are retained. 24. But <u>Thomas</u>, one of the twelve, called Didymus, <u>was not with them</u> when Jesus came. 25. The other disciples therefore said unto him, We have seen the Lord. But he said unto them, Except I shall see in his hands the print of the nails, and put my finger into the

Table 11 (continued)			
Matthew 28	Mark 16:14	Luke 24:36-40	John 20:25-28
			print of the nails, and thrust my hand into his side, I will not believe.
NOTE: Eight days after his first appearance, Jesus appeared to the apostles in Jerusalem again. Thomas was present. Jesus told the apostles to not leave Jerusalem until they received the Holy Spirit (Mark 14:14-18, Luke 24:36-53 and John 20:26-31 on pages 103-106).	14. Afterward he appeared unto the eleven as they sat at meat, and upbraided them with their unbelief and hardness of heart, because they believed not them which had seen him after he was risen.	36. And as they thus spake, Jesus himself stood in the midst of them, and saith unto them, Peace be unto you. 37. But they were terrified and affrighted, and supposed that they had seen a spirit. 38. And he said unto them, Why are ye troubled? and why do thoughts arise in your hearts? 39. Behold my hands and my feet, that it is I myself: handle me, and see; for a spirit hath not flesh and bones, as ye see me have. 40. And when he had thus spoken, he shewed them his hands and his feet.	26. And after eight days again his disciples were within, and Thomas with them: then came Jesus, the doors being shut, and stood in the midst, and said, Peace be unto you. 27. Then saith he to Thomas, Reach hither thy finger, and behold my hands; and reach hither thy hand, and thrust it into my side: and be not faithless, but believing. 28. And Thomas answered and said

| Table 11 (continued) | | | |
Matthew 28	Mark 16	Luke 24:41-46	John 20:28-31
			unto him, My Lord and my God.
			29. Jesus saith unto him, Thomas, because thou hast seen me, thou hast believed: blessed are they that have not seen, and yet have believed.
		41. And while they yet believed not for joy, and wondered, he said unto them, Have ye here any meat?	
		42. And they gave him a piece of a broiled fish, and of an honeycomb.	
		43. And he took it, and did eat before them.	30. And many other signs truly did Jesus in the presence of his disciples, which are not written in this book:
			31. But these are written, that ye might believe that Jesus is the Christ, the Son of God; and that believing ye might have life through his name.
		44. And he said unto them, These are the words which I spake unto you, while I was yet with you, that all things must be fulfilled, which were written in the law of Moses, and in the prophets, and in the psalms, concerning me.	
		45. Then opened he their understanding, that they might understand the scriptures,	
		46. And said unto them, Thus it is written,	

Table 11 (continued)

Matthew 28	Mark 16:15-18	Luke 24:46-50	John 20
		and thus it behoved Christ to suffer, and to rise from the dead the third day:	
		47. And that repentance and remission of sins should be preached in his name among all nations, beginning at Jerusalem.	
		48. And ye are witnesses of these things.	
	15. And he said unto them, Go ye into all the world, and preach the gospel to every creature.		
	16. He that believeth and is baptized shall be saved; but he that believeth not shall be damned.		
	17. And these signs shall follow them that believe; In my name shall they cast out devils; they shall speak with new tongues;		
	18. They shall take up serpents; and if they drink any deadly thing, it shall not hurt them; they shall lay hands on the sick, and they shall recover.		
		49. And, behold, I send the promise of my Father upon you: but tarry ye in the city of Jerusalem, until ye be endued with power from on high.	
		50. And he led them out as far as to Bethany, and he lifted up his hands, and blessed them.	

Table 11 (continued)			
Matthew 28:16	Mark 16	Luke 24:51-53	John 21:1-4
		51. And it came to pass, while he blessed them, he was parted from them, and carried up into heaven. 52. And they worshipped him, and returned to Jerusalem with great joy: 53. And were continually in the temple, praising and blessing God. Amen.	
The Day of Pentecost occurs.			
16. Then the eleven disciples went away into Galilee, **NOTE:** Jesus' disciples received the Holy Spirit on the day of Pentecost (Acts 2:1-4). So, some time after the day of Pentecost, the apostles left Jerusalem and went to Galilee where Jesus appeared to them the third time at the sea of Tiberias (Matthew 28:16 first part, John 21:1-25, notice verse 14). The sea of Tiberias, also called the sea of Galilee (John 6:1), is located on the eastern coast of Galilee.			1. AFTER these things Jesus shewed himself again to the disciples at the sea of Tiberias; and on this wise shewed he himself. 2. There were together Simon Peter, and Thomas called Didymus, and Nathanael of Cana in Galilee, and the sons of Zebedee, and two other of his disciples. 3. Simon Peter saith unto them, I go a fishing. They say unto him, We also go with thee. They went forth, and entered into a ship immediately; and that night they caught nothing. 4. But when morning was now come, Jesus stood on the shore: but the disciples knew not that it was Jesus.

106

Table 11 (continued)

Matthew 28	Mark 16	Luke 24	John 21:5-11
			5. Then Jesus saith unto them, Children, have ye any meat? They answered him, No.
			6. And he said unto them, Cast the net on the right side of the ship, and ye shall find. They cast therefore, and now they were not able to draw it for the multitude of fishes.
			7. Therefore that disciple whom Jesus loved saith unto Peter, It is the Lord. Now when Simon Peter heard that it was the Lord, he girt his fisher's coat unto him, (for he was naked,) and did cast himself into the sea.
			8. And the other disciples came in a little ship; (for they were not far from land, but as it were two hundred cubits,) dragging the net with fishes.
			9. As soon then as they were come to land, they saw a fire of coals there, and fish laid thereon, and bread.
			10. Jesus saith unto them, Bring of the fish which ye have now caught.
			11. Simon Peter went up, and drew the net to land full of great fishes, an hundred and fifty and three: and for all there were so many, yet was not

Table 11 (continued)			
Matthew 28	Mark 16	Luke 24	John 21:11-17
			the net broken.
			12. Jesus saith unto them, Come and dine. And none of the disciples durst ask him, Who art thou? knowing that it was the Lord.
			13. Jesus then cometh, and taketh bread, and giveth them, and fish likewise.
			14. This is now the **third time** that <u>Jesus shewed himself to his disciples</u>, after that he was risen from the dead.
			15. So when they had dined, Jesus saith to Simon Peter, Simon, son of Jonas, lovest thou me more than these? He saith unto him, Yea, Lord; thou knowest that I love thee. He saith unto him, Feed my lambs.
			16. He saith to him again the second time, Simon, son of Jonas, lovest thou me? He saith unto him, Yea, Lord; thou knowest that I love thee. He saith unto him, Feed my sheep.
			17. He saith unto him the third time, Simon, son of Jonas, lovest thou me? Peter was grieved because he said unto him the third time, Lovest thou me? And he said unto him, Lord, thou knowest all things; thou

Table 11 (continued)			
Matthew 28	Mark 16	Luke 24	John 21:17-24
			knowest that I love thee. Jesus saith unto him, Feed my sheep.
			18. Verily, verily, I say unto thee, When thou wast young, thou girdedst thyself, and walkedst whither thou wouldest: but when thou shalt be old, thou shalt stretch forth thy hands, and another shall gird thee, and carry thee whither thou wouldest not.
			19. This spake he, signifying by what death he should glorify God. And when he had spoken this, he saith unto him, Follow me.
			20. Then Peter, turning about, seeth the disciple whom Jesus loved following; which also leaned on his breast at supper, and said, Lord, which is he that betrayeth thee?
			21. Peter seeing him saith to Jesus, Lord, and what shall this man do?
			22. Jesus saith unto him, If I will that he tarry till I come, what is that to thee? follow thou me.
			23. Then went this saying abroad among the brethren, that that disciple should not die: yet Jesus said not unto him, He shall not die; but, If I will that he tarry till I come, what is that to thee?
			24. This is the disciple which testifieth of

Table 11 (continued)			
Matthew 28:16-20	Mark 16:19	Luke 24	John 21:24-25
			these things, and wrote these things: and we know that his testimony is true. 25. And there are also many other things which Jesus did, the which, if they should be written every one, I suppose that even the world itself could not contain the books that should be written. Amen.
16. . . . into a mountain (in Galilee - see the first part of this verse on page 106) where Jesus had appointed them. 17. And when they saw him, they worshipped him: but some doubted. 18. And Jesus came and spake unto them, saying, All power is given unto me in heaven and in earth. 19. Go ye therefore, and teach all nations, baptizing them in the name of the Father, and of the Son, and of the Holy Ghost: 20. Teaching them to observe all things whatsoever I have commanded you: and, lo, I am with you alway, even unto the end of the world. Amen.			**NOTE**: After Jesus' third appearance, the eleven apostles went to a mountain in Galilee where Jesus appeared to them the fourth time and told them to go and teach all nations (Matthew 28:16-20, Mark 16:19-20 on pages 110-111).
	19. So then after the Lord had spoken unto them, he was received up into heaven, and sat on the right hand of God.		

Table 11 (continued)			
Matthew 28	Mark 16:20	Luke 24	John 21
	20. And they went forth, and preached every where, the Lord working with them, and confirming the word with signs following. Amen.		

Chapter 12

What Have We Learned?

Chapter 11 completes the discussion of the betrayal, death and resurrection of Jesus Christ so let's review what we've learned. In Chapter 2 we saw that God has recorded certain events in all four gospel accounts which, in effect, divide Matthew, Mark, Luke and John into definite periods of time, periods of time which begin with an event recorded in all four gospel accounts and end with the next event recorded in all four gospel accounts. The statements and events recorded in Matthew, Mark, Luke and John are interrelated and have to be studied together and compared, then put together in the correct time sequence to fully understand what happened. By doing this, we learned that:

* Jesus discussed his betrayal two different times during the passover meal in the goodman's house, the first time before the symbolic bread and wine were given, the second time after the bread and wine were given (pages 14-18).
* In the goodman's house, Jesus prophesied that before the rooster crowed Peter would deny him three times (page 21).
* After Jesus and the apostles left the goodman's house, Jesus told Peter again that before the rooster crowed, Peter would deny him three times. When Peter argued with him, Jesus added the prophecy that before the rooster crowed <u>twice</u>, Peter would deny him three (more) times (page 35).
* Peter denied Jesus six times just as Jesus had said he would (pages 47-51, 58-59).
* In Gethsemane, the angel appeared to Jesus during his second prayer (page 37).
* Pilate tried desperately to release Jesus (pages 70-71).
* Jesus was scourged twice, not once, before he was crucified (pages 68 and 72).
* The tearing of the veil in the temple began at the top in the middle of the veil when Jesus said, "It is finished," and ended at the bottom of the veil right after he died (page 82).
* Jesus died and was buried on a Wednesday afternoon, shortly before sunset. God the Father resurrected him late in the afternoon on Saturday, exactly three days and three nights after his body was placed in the tomb. By the time the women arrived at the tomb on Sunday morning, Jesus was already risen. He had been resurrected and had been alive again for approximately twelve hours (pages 91-93).
* The gospels show Jesus appeared to the apostles, as a group, four times after his resurrection: the first two times in Jerusalem, the third and fourth times in Galilee (page 102).

We've also learned that Bible study can be very hard work, requiring considerable thought and effort and that its easy to think the Bible contradicts itself when it doesn't. God inspired the Bible to be written and God is not the author of confusion or contradiction.

<u>II Timothy 2:15</u>
15. Study to shew thyself approved unto God, a <u>workman</u> that needeth not to be ashamed, rightly dividing the word of truth.

<u>II Timothy 3:16-17</u>
16. <u>All scripture</u> is given <u>by inspiration of God</u>, and is profitable for doctrine, for reproof, for

correction, for instruction in righteousness:

17. That the man of God may be perfect, throughly furnished unto all good works.

I Corinthians 14:33

33. For <u>God is not the author of confusion</u>, but of peace, as in all churches of the saints.

In John 10:35 Jesus plainly stated the scriptures cannot be broken, or all of the scriptures must agree. So when scriptures appear to contradict each other, instead of immediately thinking that the Bible contradicts itself, we need to realize we probably just don't understand those scriptures yet.

In writing the gospels, I believe God inspired four different men to write or develop "four pieces of a puzzle." When these puzzle pieces are put together correctly, they tell the surprising story of the betrayal, death and resurrection of Jesus Christ. I don't believe that any man, of himself, nor any group of men, of themselves, would have written the gospels the way they are written. Think about it! Matthew 27:21-23, Mark 15:12-14 and Luke 23:18-23 on pages 70-71 describe the argument Pilate had with the multitude about releasing Jesus. If men, of themselves, had written this account, I don't believe they would have placed this information in three separate books. They would have placed all of this information in one book, in sequential order, so that it might be more easily understood. But God inspired the gospels to be written in a way that would keep their full understanding a <u>secret</u> until the time he wanted it understood.

Deuteronomy 29:29

29. The secret things belong unto the Lord our God: but those things which are revealed belong unto us and to our children for ever, that we may do all the words of this law.

For whatever reasons, God has waited until now to show us how Matthew, Mark, Luke and John are written and how they should be studied. And through this study, God has granted us basic understanding that I believe will ultimately affect the beliefs and lives of every Christian.

NOTE: If you have comments, questions or require further information please write: Michael C. Nichols, P. O. Box 3850, Peachtree City, Georgia, 30269.

Chapter 13

Paraphrase

The following story is a paraphrase of the events recorded in the tables in Chapters 3 through 11. This story tells what really happened from the time Jesus told his disciples to prepare the passover meal to the time the apostles left Galilee to go into the world to teach. The numbers in parentheses are page numbers in this book. You can use these numbers to refer to the scriptures in the tables and verify the accuracy of this story (i.e. the events described between (12) and (13) can be found on page 12 of this book).

Preparing the Passover Meal

(12) As the passover approached, the disciples asked Jesus where he would like to have the meal. Jesus told Peter and John to go into the city (13) where they would meet a man carrying a pitcher of water. They were to follow that man to whatever house he entered and tell the owner of the house that Jesus wanted to celebrate the passover at that home with his disciples.

Peter and John did as they were told and, indeed, encountered a man carrying a pitcher of water. Events unfolded just as Jesus had predicted and the homeowner showed the two disciples an "upper room" that was furnished and available for their use.

The First Discussion of Jesus' Betrayal

In the evening Jesus and the disciples walked to the home where they would have their passover meal. Before dinner began, Jesus said, "It's very important to me that I eat this passover meal with you before my sacrifice. And I want you to know that I won't eat it again until we eat it together in the kingdom of God." (14) Then after giving the disciples

a container of wine to be divided among themselves, Jesus said, "I also want you to know that I won't drink wine again until the kingdom of God has come."

As they were eating, Jesus continued to surprise the disciples with predictions of impending events. When Jesus said, "One of you at this table will betray me," the disciples were stunned and very upset. Then each disciple, one by one, asked Jesus, "Lord, am I the one? . . . Is it me? . . . You can't mean me." Jesus would not specifically identify the betrayer, but said only that it was one of the disciples, then warned, "What is written about the Son of man is going to happen, but it will be terrible for the one who betrays the Son of man! That man would have been better off if he had never been born." When Judas Iscariot said, "Master, you surely don't mean me." Jesus answered, "That's what you say." This totally different response to the same basic question the other disciples had asked, in all likelihood, shocked Judas greatly.

The Symbolic Bread and Wine

As they continued to eat, Jesus used unleavened bread and wine from the dinner table to establish a new way to observe the passover and honor him as the true Passover Lamb of God who would make it possible for all mankind to be given eternal salvation. This "new way," or new ceremony, is a centerpiece of commonly held beliefs among many Christian denominations.

After Jesus blessed and broke the bread, he told the disciples, "Take this and eat it because it is my body which is sacrificed for you. And (15) do this so that you will always remember what I did for you." Of course, the disciples were quite familiar with the concept of a lamb being sacrificed to God on the passover, but they did not immediately connect Jesus' words with the concept of his own personal sacrifice to God.

After the bread, Jesus took a cup of wine, gave thanks and told the disciples to all drink from the cup. After they did, Jesus said, "This wine is my blood which will be shed for your sins and the sins of many others. My shed blood is the blood on which a new covenant between God and man will be established. And as I told you earlier, I will not drink wine again until I drink it new with you in the kingdom of God."

The Footwashing

Perhaps the biggest surprise of all for the disciples that night occurred when Jesus washed their feet. As the passover meal came to an end, Judas became fully determined to betray Jesus. At this same time, Jesus' thoughts focused on God. He knew that God had given him all things. He also knew that he had come from God and that he would shortly return to God.

With these thoughts on his mind, Jesus stood at the table, removed his outer clothing and dressed himself like a domestic servant, wrapping a towel around his waist. He poured water in a large bowl and began to wash the disciples feet, and then dry them with the towel. Remember that men in Jesus' time wore shoes that left their feet exposed to the dirt, sand and filth of the streets when they walked. So Peter couldn't comprehend what he was seeing. Jesus Christ, the Son of God, his sinless leader and teacher, was washing feet like a domestic servant.

(16) When Jesus came in turn to Peter, Peter asked him, "Lord, are you going to wash my feet?" Jesus said "I know you don't understand what I'm doing now, but I'll explain a little later." Peter said, "I won't ever let you wash my feet!" Jesus responded, "If I don't wash your feet, you can't be with me." Peter replied, "Then don't just wash my feet, wash my hands and my head also." Jesus said, "A person who has bathed only needs to wash his feet, and you are clean, but not all of you." Jesus said, "Not all of you," because he knew who would betray him.

After Jesus finished washing the disciples' feet he put his clothing back on, sat down at the table again, and asked the disciples, "Do you understand what I have done? You call me your teacher and your leader, and you should, because that's what I am. So, if I, your leader and teacher, have washed your feet, you should also wash each other's feet. (17) I have set an example for you to follow. Remember, the servant is not greater than his master and the messenger is not greater than the one who sent him. If you understand these things and do them, God will bless you."

The Second Discussion of Jesus' Betrayal

Jesus continued, "I'm not talking about all of you. I know the ones I've chosen, but to fulfill the scripture, 'He who has eaten bread with me has turned against me.' I am telling you this before it actually happens, so that when it happens, you'll believe that I am ("I am" is the most holy name for God)."

"Now listen carefully, anyone who receives those I send, receives me. Anyone who receives me, receives the one who sent me." After saying this, Jesus was deeply troubled and said, "Look, the hand of my betrayer lies with my hand at this moment on the table. I'm telling you the truth, one of you will betray me. (18) The Son of man will die in the way that has already been determined, but it will be terrible for the man who betrays him." The disciples looked at each other, wondering who the betrayer was, then began to ask each other who was going to do this.

Jesus Identifies Judas Iscariot As His Betrayer

Since John was leaning next to Jesus, Peter motioned to John to ask Jesus who the betrayer was. John asked Jesus, and Jesus said, "I will give this food to him after I have dipped it in the gravy." After Jesus gave Judas Iscariot the food, Satan entered Judas, and Jesus told him, "What you're going to do, do quickly." No one at the table understood why Jesus said this, but (19) since Judas was responsible for the group's money, some assumed that Jesus told him to buy the things they needed for the feast or to give something to the poor. As soon as Judas received the food, he went out into the night.

The Disciples Argue Over Who Will Be The Greatest

After Judas left and Jesus spoke of being glorified, the disciples argued about which one of them would be the greatest. Jesus told them, "Foreign kings 'lord it over their people' and kings who use authority in this way call themselves everyone's friend. But you will not rule as they do! As a leader, you must deeply respect those who follow you; you must treat them as a younger person treats his elders; you must be a servant to them. Now I want you to think about who is greater, the person who sits at the table and eats, or the person who serves him? Isn't it the one eating? (20) But I am among you as a servant.

"Now since you have stayed with me during all my trials, I have given you positions of leadership in the kingdom my Father has given me, so that we can eat and drink together and you can sit on thrones judging the twelve tribes of Israel.

"Simon! Simon! Listen to me! Satan wants to really test each one of you, but I've asked the Father to strengthen your faith and after you receive his Holy Spirit, help the others.

Jesus Prophesies that Peter Will Deny Him Three Times

"Little children, I won't be with you much longer. You'll look for me, but as I told the Jews, you can't go where I'm going. But before I leave, I'm giving you a new commandment. Love each other - love each other as I have loved you - and then everyone will know that you're my disciples.

(21) Peter interrupted, "Lord, where are you going?" Jesus answered, "You can't go with me now, but you will later." Peter asked, "Why can't I go with you? I'm ready to go to jail with you. I'm even willing to die for you." Jesus asked, "Would you really die for me? Peter, I'm telling you the truth, before the rooster crows today, you'll say that you don't know me three times."

The Final Conversation in the House

Then Jesus said, "I don't want you to worry or be afraid. You have faith in God, so have faith in me.

"In my Father's kingdom are many places or positions. I wouldn't tell you this, if it wasn't true. Your places within this kingdom are as rulers of the tribes or nations of Israel. I'm going away to 'prepare your place.' What I mean by this is that, first, I'll prepare you to lead your nations. But as the leaders of such large groups of people, you'll need help. So while I'm away, I'll also prepare others to help you. When you and all of the other leaders you will need to help you are ready, or when your "place" or positions of rulership are fully staffed with qualified leaders, I'll return so that we can all be together. Now you know where I'm going and you know the way."

(22) Thomas said, "Lord, we don't know where you're going and we don't know how to get there." Jesus answered, "I am the way, the truth, and the life. You can never meet the Father unless you become like me, unless you think like I think, and live like I live.

"If you know me, you should know my Father, because my Father and I are alike! We are the same with regard to character, love, truth and the way we live. So, if you know me, you know him; and if you've seen me, you've seen him.

Philip said, "Lord, all we need is to see the Father." Jesus answered, "Have I been with you this long, Philip, and you still don't know me? If you've seen me, you've seen the Father, so, why do you ask to see the Father? Don't you believe that the Father and I are in complete agreement? It's like we're the same person. Even the words that I speak are not my words, they are my Father's. So, believe me when I tell you that the Father and I are in complete harmony, or else believe me because of the things that I'm able to do.

"Fellows, what I'm going to tell you is true. If you have faith in me, (23) you will do all the things I've done, and more, because I'll be with the Father. Also remember that if you ask for anything in my name, I will do it. In this way, the Son will honor the Father.

"If you love me, keep my commandments; and I will ask the Father to give you the Holy Spirit to help you and be with you forever. The Holy Spirit is the Spirit of truth. The people in the world won't accept the Spirit of truth right now because they aren't truly aware that he exists, but you are, because you know he's with you and will be in you. I won't leave you helpless. I'll come back to you.

"In a little while the people in the world won't see me anymore, but you will; and because I will live again, you will too. At that time you will understand what it means to be in total harmony and agreement with me and my Father.

"By keeping my commandments, you show that you love me. (24) In return, my Father and I will love you. Also, I will reveal myself to you."

Judas (not Iscariot) asked, "How will you reveal yourself to us and not to the people in the world?" Jesus answered, "As I said, anyone who loves me will obey me. In return, my Father will love him, and my Father and I will live in him. Anyone who doesn't love me will not obey me. Remember, these are not my words - they are my Father's - and he sent me to tell you this.

"While I've been with you, I've taught you; but after I'm gone, the Holy Spirit will teach you and help you remember what I've said.

"My parting gift to you is peace - peace of mind. My peace isn't fragile and temporary like the peace in this world. My peace lasts. So don't worry and don't be afraid.

"You've heard me say that I was going away and then coming back (25) to you. If you love me, you will be happy because I'm going to the Father, and the Father is more powerful than I am. I'm telling you this before it happens, so that when it happens, you will believe that I am.

"In the past, when I sent you out to teach and you had no money, no food and no shoes, did you need anything?" They said, "No." Jesus said, "Now its different. If you have money and food, take them. If you don't have a sword, then sell some clothing if you have to, and buy one. For the scripture says that I will be condemned as a criminal, and the things written about me will certainly happen." When some of the disciples said, "Lord, we have two swords," Jesus said, "Two swords are enough."

Then Jesus said, "I won't be talking with you much anymore because the ruler of this world is coming. And even though he doesn't influence me, he will be allowed to do things to me that will prove to the world (26) how much I love the Father and that I will obey the Father no matter what. Let's get up now and leave." After Jesus and the disciples sang a hymn, they left the house and walked to the mount of Olives.

Jesus and the Disciples Walk to the Mount of Olives

(27&28) As Jesus and the disciples walked to the mount of Olives, Jesus was in deep thought about the crucifixion and the decision he had to make - would he willingly lay down his life, or would he ask his Father to save him? But from time to time, when an important thought would "hit his mind" he would share it with his disciples.

Jesus said, "I am the true vine, and my Father is the gardener. He cuts away every branch in me that doesn't bear fruit. He trims clean every branch that bears fruit, so that it will bear more fruit. Right now, you are like branches that have been trimmed clean because of what I've taught you. So stay attached to me and I'll stay attached to you, and you will bear fruit. If you don't stay attached to me, you'll be thrown aside like a branch. You'll wither, be gathered, thrown in the fire and burned. I am the vine; you are the branches. Without me you can do nothing. But if you let my words live in you, you will be given whatever you ask for; you will prove to me that you are my disciples; and you will bear abundant fruit and honor my Father.

"I have loved you as my Father loves me. Don't let this change! If you obey me, I will continue to love you, even as I obey my Father and he continues to love me. I'm telling you these things so that you can be as happy as I am.

"I command you to love each other as I have loved you. No one can show greater love than by giving his life for his friends. And you are my friends if you obey me. I won't call you servants anymore (29) because a servant doesn't know what his master is doing. But I will call you friends because I have told you everything my Father has told me.

"You didn't choose me. I chose you and I expect you to bear fruit that lasts, so that the Father will give you whatever you ask for in my name.

"If you do the things I command, you'll learn how to love each other.

"If the people in the world hate you, remember that they hated me first. If you lived as the people in the world live, they would love you. But since I chose you and you don't live like they do, they hate you. Do you remember when I said that the servant isn't greater than his master? It's true. So since they've persecuted me, they'll persecute you. If they had done what I said, they would do what you say. And they'll hate and persecute (30) you because of who I am and because they don't know my Father.

"If I hadn't come and told them that what they were doing was wrong, I wouldn't be able to hold them responsible, but now I can. If they hadn't ignored the things I did - things that no one else ever did - I wouldn't have known how much they hated me. And whoever hates me also hates my Father. So by ignoring the things I did, they proved that they know me and my Father, and hate us both. Their actions fulfill the scripture that states, 'They hated me without a cause.'

"When I send you the Spirit of truth from the Father, he will tell you about me. And you will also tell others about me because you have been with me from the beginning.

"I've told you these things so that when they mistreat you, you won't let their actions cause you to hate the Father and me. They're going to throw you out of the synagogues and (31) even kill some of you, and all the while think they're serving God. And they'll do these things because they're deceived and have

no idea what my Father and I are really like. I've also told you these things, so that when they happen, you'll remember that I warned you. And I didn't tell you these things at first, because I was with you.

"All of you know I'm leaving, but none of you has asked me where I'm going. And I can tell that what I've told you has made you sad. But you need to understand that what I'm doing is for your good. If I don't go away, you won't be given the Holy Spirit, but if I go away, I'll send him to you. Now when he comes, he'll ultimately show the people in the world they are wrong with regard to sin, righteousness and judgment.

"With regard to sin, the Spirit of truth will show the people in the world that they are guilty of the sin of unbelief because they simply don't believe me.

"With regard to righteousness, I'm going to the Father and you won't see (32) me any more. You'll learn, as the people in the world will, that it's harder to do the right thing when I'm not present with you and you can't see me.

"With regard to judgment, the ruler of the people in this world is judged. The people will ultimately see that they have been worshipping the god of this world, Satan, and not the true God.

"I have a lot more to teach you, but you're not ready yet. So the Spirit will teach you when he comes. He will tell you what I tell him to, and he will tell you things that will happen in the future. He will honor me because he will give you what is mine. Anything the Spirit gives you is mine because all that the Father has belongs to me.

"You won't see me for a little while. Then a little later, you'll see me again, because I go to the Father." Some of the disciples asked each other, "What is he saying? You won't see me for a little while, then a little later, you'll see me again, and because I go to the Father? We don't understand what he's talking about!" (33) Jesus knew they had some questions, so he asked them if they wanted him to explain what he meant. They said they did, so he told them, "You'll cry and be sad while the world rejoices. You'll be sad, then later, you'll be happy. A woman in childbirth is in great pain, but as soon as the child is born, the joy she experiences helps her forget the pain. Right now, you're like women in childbirth; you're sad. But when I see you again, you'll be so happy that no one will be able to make you sad.

"When I'm alive again, you won't ask me for anything. You'll ask the Father himself, but you'll ask in my name. That's the same as if I had asked him, so he will give you whatever you ask for.

(34) "Up until now I've used parables or examples a lot when I've talked to you, but in the future I won't. I'll speak plainly.

"I left the Father and came into the world. Now, I'm leaving the world and returning to the Father." His disciples said, "Now you are speaking plainly and not using examples. Now we know that you know all things and that no one has to ask you something for you to understand what they're thinking. Because of this, we believe you came from God."

Jesus asked, "Do you really think you believe now?"

Jesus Prophesies That Peter Will Deny Him Six Times

(35) "Listen to me! In the future . . . no . . . in just a few hours, all of you will be scattered and go back to your own homes. You'll desert me! But I won't be alone, because the Father is with me. All of you will be frightened by what will happen to me tonight, because the scripture states, 'I will kill the shepherd and the sheep will be scattered!' But after I'm resurrected I'll meet you in Galilee." Peter responded, "Even if everyone else is frightened, I won't be." Jesus said, "Peter, this very night, before the rooster crows, you'll say that you don't know me three times."

Peter argued, "Even if everyone else is frightened, I won't be." Jesus responded, "During this day, no, this very night, before the rooster crows twice, you'll say that you don't know me three times." (36) Peter continued to argue, "Even if I have to die with you, I won't deny you in any way." Then all of the other disciples said the same thing.

Just before Jesus and the disciples arrived at Gethsemane where Jesus would become weighted down with sorrow and depressing thoughts, he offered the disciples encouragement saying, "I've told you these things so that you can have peace of mind. You will have trials and problems in this world, but be encouraged because I have overcome the world."

Jesus' Three Prayers In Gethsemane

When Jesus and his disciples arrived in Gethsemane, Jesus told the disciples to sit while he went and prayed. He took Peter, James and John deeper into the garden with him asking the others to wait behind. Jesus explained to the three with him that he was very sad and asked them to stay with him and help him watch. Jesus walked a short distance from them, fell face-down on the ground and asked his Father (37) if there was any way he could avoid the awful death he was about to endure.

When Jesus returned from his first prayer, he found the disciples sleeping. He asked Peter, "Simon, are you sleeping? Couldn't you watch one hour?" He told the disciples, "Watch and pray, so that you won't be tempted. The spirit is willing, but your flesh is weak."

Jesus left again and went about a stone's throw from them. This time he kneeled down and prayed again that his Father would save him from being crucified, but that, of course, God's will be done. An angel appeared to strengthen Jesus and he prayed so earnestly that his sweat was like great drops of blood falling to the ground.

When he returned and found the disciples sleeping again, (38) he asked, "Why are you sleeping?" The disciples didn't know what to answer. Jesus told them, "Rise and pray, so that you won't be tempted."

Jesus left to pray the third time. In his third prayer he asked again that his Father save him from being crucified. Then he stopped, and thought about God, mankind, and God's plan of salvation for mankind and, with God's help, decided to give his life for the sins of mankind. After he made this decision, he looked up to heaven and said,

"Father its time to honor your Son, that your Son can honor you. I can honor you because you have given me the authority over all mankind to decide who will be given eternal life. To receive eternal life, mankind must come to know you, the only true God, and Jesus Christ, the one you sent. I have honored you on the earth by doing everything you gave me to do. Now honor me, Father, in your presence and give me back the glory that I had with you before the world was created.

(39) "I've told my disciples about you. These are men you chose from this world and led to me, and they have obeyed you. They know that you gave me everything I have. I told them what you told me to tell them, and they believed me. They know that I came from you and that you sent me. I am praying for them, but not for those who belong to this world. My disciples belong to you, so I am praying for them. Everyone that I have is yours, and everyone that you have is mine, and my disciples will bring honor to me.

"I'm just about ready to leave this world and come back to you, but my disciples will stay here. Holy Father, keep these people together by your power - the power in your name - so that they can be in unity as we are. While I was with them, I kept them together by your power. And they are still together, (40) except for the one who left, the son of destruction - the child of Satan - that the scripture could be fulfilled.

"I'll be with you shortly, but I ask these things now, so that my disciples can be as happy as I am. I've told them what you told me to tell them, and they believed me. Now, the people in the world hate them because they don't belong to the world, just as I don't. Father, I'm not asking that you take them out of the world. I'm asking that you keep them from the evil one.

"Help them become like me by giving them an understanding of the truth. Your word is truth.

"I'm going to send them into the world, just as you sent me. And for their sakes I will sacrifice my life so that you can give them an understanding of the truth. And I'm not praying just for these disciples. I'm also praying for everyone else who will believe in me because of what these disciples will tell them. I want all of them to be in harmony and agreement with each other as you and I are. I also want them to be in total agreement with us. Then the people of this world will believe (41) that you sent me.

"I have given them the knowledge and understanding you told me to give them, so that they can be in unity as we are. With you living in me, and me living in them, they can grow to a point of total agreement with us, and the world can know that you have sent me, and have loved them and me.

"Father, I also ask that my disciples be with me so they can see my glory, and know you loved me before the world was created.

"Righteous Father, the world doesn't know you, but I know you, and my disciples know that you sent me. I've told them about you and I will continue to tell them about you, so that your love for me can be in them and that I myself can live in them.

Jesus Is Taken Captive

After his third prayer, Jesus returned to his disciples (42) and found them asleep again, but this time he didn't wake them up. After he let them sleep a while, Jesus said, "You've slept long enough, wake up; its time for the Son of Man to be betrayed and taken captive by evil men. Get up, we've got to go." After Jesus and the disciples crossed over the brook Cedron, they entered a garden that Judas knew about. As Jesus and the disciples entered the garden, Jesus said "Look, my betrayer is here," just as Judas arrived with a large group of armed men.

(43) Jesus already knew everything that was going to happen, so he approached the group of men and asked who they were looking for. When they answered, "Jesus of Nazareth," Jesus said, "I am." Judas was standing with the group and as soon as Jesus said, "I am," the whole group of men stepped back and fell to the ground. Jesus asked them again who they were looking for. When they said Jesus of Nazareth again, Jesus said, "I told you that I am. If I'm the one you're looking for, let these others go."

(44) Judas had told those with him, "The

one I will kiss is the man you want. Take him and lead him away." When Jesus approached the group again, Judas went right to him and said, "Master, Master," and kissed him. After Jesus asked Judas why he was there, he asked him if he was using a kiss to betray him.

When the disciples saw some of the men grab Jesus, they asked Jesus if he wanted them to fight with their swords. Without waiting for an answer, Peter drew a sword and cut off the right ear of the high priest's servant. The servant's name was Malchus. Jesus stopped the fight and healed Malchus' ear. (45) He told Peter, "Put your sword away, for everyone who lives by the sword will die by the sword. I must drink from the cup that my Father has given me. Don't you know that if I asked, my Father would send more than twelve legions of angels to save me? But if I asked to be saved, how would the scriptures be fulfilled concerning what should happen to me?"

Then Jesus asked the Jewish leaders who were there, "Why have you come with weapons to arrest me like a criminal? I was with you in the temple every day and you didn't try to arrest me then. But you've been given the power to do this at this time by the god of this world."

Then all of the disciples left Jesus and ran away. One of them was a young man who was wearing only a linen cloth. When the (46) men in the group grabbed him, he left the linen cloth behind and ran away naked.

After Jesus was arrested and tied up, he was taken to Annas, the father-in-law of Caiaphas. Caiaphas was the high priest that same year and it was Caiaphas who had told the Jewish leaders that it was better for them if one man died for the people. After they saw Annas, they took Jesus to Caiaphas' house where all the chief priests, elders and scribes were gathered. Peter and John followed. Since John knew the high priest, he was allowed to enter the courtyard with Jesus, but Peter stood outside near the gate.

The Trial and the Six Denials

(47) After John came back out and spoke to the girl who tended the gate of the courtyard,

Peter was allowed to come in. But as Peter entered, the girl asked him if he was one of Jesus' disciples. Peter said he wasn't. This was Peter's first denial. It was cold that night, so someone had built a fire in the middle of the courtyard. After standing by the fire for a few minutes, Peter and some of the servants and officers were able to find different things to sit on, so they could sit by the fire and warm themselves and watch what would happen.

(48) The high priest questioned Jesus about his disciples and his teachings. Jesus told him, "I've spoken publicly to everyone. I've taught in our meeting places and in the temple where all the Jews gather. I've said nothing in secret! Why are you asking me these things? Ask those who heard me; they know what I said." Then one of the temple officers hit Jesus in the face with the palm of his hand and said, "That's no way to talk to the high priest!" Jesus answered, "If I've done something wrong, tell me, but if I haven't, why did you hit me?" Jesus was tied up when Annas sent him to Caiaphas and he was still tied up while he was questioned.

The chief priests, elders and all the counsel wanted to put Jesus to death, so they tried to find people who would lie about Jesus in a mock trial. And even though many people came and lied, what they said didn't agree. Then two men came forward (49) and said that Jesus had made the following statements, "I can destroy the temple of God and rebuild it in three days," and "I will destroy this temple that is made with hands and within three days, I'll build another temple that is made without hands." So their testimony didn't agree either.

When Jesus didn't respond, the high priest stood up and asked, "Why don't you say something in your own defense? Don't you hear what these people are saying?" When Jesus still didn't answer, the high priest said, "I command you by the living God to tell us if you are the Christ, the Son of God." Jesus didn't respond, so the high priest asked again, "Are you the Christ, the Son of the Blessed?" Jesus replied, "That's what you say, and I am, and in the future you will see the Son of Man sitting on the right hand of power and coming in the clouds of heaven." When he heard this, the high priest tore his clothes and verbally exploded, saying, "This is blasphemy for he claims to be God! (50) Do we need any more witnesses? You heard what he said. What do you think?" The others said that Jesus was guilty and deserved to die. Then some of these men spit on Jesus. Others covered his face and hit him, then said, "Prophesy unto us, you Christ. Who hit you?"

As Jesus was mocked and beaten, Peter sat outside in the courtyard by the fire. A maid who was stationed in the courtyard, came up to him. After she stared at him, she told him, "You were also with Jesus of Galilee." She then told the others who were gathered by the fire that Peter was with Jesus. Peter denied it. This was Peter's second denial. Apparently Peter felt uncomfortable staying by the fire, so he went out into the porch. (51) There, another maid told those on the porch that Peter was also with Jesus. Peter swore that he didn't know Jesus. This was Peter's third denial. (58) After his third denial, the rooster crowed the first time.

Peter came back into the courtyard from the porch and stood by the fire again to warm himself. The maid in the courtyard saw him again and told the people standing by the fire that Peter was one of Jesus' disciples. The people asked Peter, "Aren't you also one of his disciples?" Peter said, "I am not!" This was Peter's fourth denial. Peter was trapped. It seemed that no matter where he went, he ran into another person who thought he was Jesus' disciple.

After his fourth denial, Peter walked away from the fire, but stayed in the courtyard where, a little later, a lone male told him, "You are also one of them." Peter said, "Man, I am not." This was Peter's fifth denial.

About an hour later, those who had earlier stood by the fire with Peter, came to Peter in the courtyard. After one of them said, "We know that you are one of them because you talk like someone from Galilee," (59) another added, "You've got to be one of his disciples; your Galilean accent gives you away." One of the high priest's servants was also in the group. He was a relative of Malchus, whose ear Peter had cut off, and he said, "Didn't I see you in the garden with him?" As this man thought about it, he realized he had seen Peter and boldly stated, "I know what I'm talking about, this man was with Jesus, for he is a Galilean." Peter replied, "Man, I don't know what you're saying. I don't even know the man you're talking about!" After this sixth denial, the rooster crowed the second time, and Jesus turned and looked at Peter. Then Peter remembered that Jesus had said he would deny him three times before the rooster crowed. Peter left the courtyard and cried hard. (60) As he cried, he remembered that Jesus had also said that he would deny him three more times before the rooster crowed twice. As Peter thought about these things, he continued to cry.

Pilate

(61) As Peter wept outside, the men who were guarding Jesus made fun of him. They also blindfolded him, hit him, and told him, "Tell us who hit you." At daybreak, after the Jewish leaders met privately and decided to put Jesus to death, they brought Jesus into the meeting and asked him, "Are you the Messiah, tell us." Jesus answered, "If I tell you, you won't believe me. If I ask you anything, you won't answer me, and you won't let me go. (62) But from now on the Son of Man will be seated on the right hand of God." Then the council members asked, "Are you the Son of God?" Jesus said, "You say that I am." And they said, "We don't need any more evidence. He just confessed." After the council members tied Jesus up, they took him to the building where Pontius Pilate stayed. But the Jews wouldn't go into the building. If they did, they would be ceremonially defiled and therefore unable to eat the passover.

Judas Iscariot had been lurking nearby and when he learned that Jesus was sentenced to death, he returned the thirty pieces of silver to the priests and said, "I've sinned because I've betrayed an innocent man." When the priests said, "So what? That's your problem," Judas threw the silver down and went out and hanged himself.

(63) When the Jews arrived with Jesus, Pilate went out and asked them what charges

they were bringing against this man. When the Jews wouldn't give specific charges, Pilate told them to judge Jesus themselves. After saying they weren't allowed to put any man to death, (64) they accused Jesus of attempting to incite riots, telling people to not pay taxes and claiming to be a king. When Pilate heard this, he went back inside and asked Jesus, "Are you the King of the Jews?" Jesus asked, "Are you asking me this on your own or did someone else say this about me?" Pilate responded, "Look, I'm not a Jew, your own people and the chief priests brought you to me. What have you done to make them so mad?" Jesus answered, "My kingdom is not a part of this world. If it were, my disciples would have fought to keep me from being arrested." (65) Pilate asked, "So, are you a king?" Jesus answered, "You are saying that I am a king. That is why I was born and why I came to teach the truth. Those who understand the truth hear what I say."

As Pilate turned to walk out and speak to the Jews, he asked, "What is truth?"

When Pilate told the Jews that he thought Jesus was innocent, they became furious, saying that Jesus had been stirring up all kinds of trouble from Galilee to Jerusalem with his teachings. When Jesus didn't respond to their accusations, Pilate said, "Don't you hear what they're saying?" When Jesus didn't utter a word, Pilate was shocked and (66) asked again, "Why don't you answer? Don't you hear what they're saying about you?" When Jesus still said nothing, Pilate couldn't believe it.

When Pilate heard that Jesus had taught in Gallilee, he asked if Jesus was a Galilean. Galilee was an area of the region that was notorious for its riotous and rebellious residents. So Pilate took this opportunity to see if he could find a way out of his dilemma. Since Herod was the Jewish-born politician responsible for governing Galilee and Herod was in Jerusalem at the time, Pilate referred the case to Herod. The solution was simple: dump the problem on Herod.

Herod had heard a lot about Jesus and had wanted to see him for a long time. So he was very happy when he finally got his chance. Herod thought Jesus might even perform a miracle for him. When Jesus arrived, the following things happened: Herod asked Jesus a lot of questions, but Jesus didn't answer; the chief priests and scribes accused Jesus of many bad things; and Herod and his soldiers made fun of Jesus and humiliated him. After Herod had Jesus dressed in a gorgeous robe, he sent him back to Pilate. That same day Herod and Pilate (67) became friends. Before that, they were enemies.

Jesus' trial was taking place during the Jewish Passover season and it was traditional for Pilate to release one Jewish prisoner chosen by the people. Since Pilate knew that the chief priests had delivered Jesus because of jealousy, he hoped he could convince the people to set Jesus free. After Jesus was returned from Herod, Pilate asked the crowd, "Which prisoner do you want me to release, Barabbas or Jesus?" The chief priests told those in the crowd to choose Barabbas. (68) Pilate asked again who they wanted him to release and asked specifically if they wanted him to release Jesus. The crowd cried out again, "Not Jesus, but Barabbas." Now Barabbas was a robber.

Pilate responded, "You brought this man to me and told me he was a criminal. But I have questioned him here in front of you and I haven't found him guilty of anything you said. And Herod agrees with me. So, I will just scourge him and release him." Pilate sat down on the judgment seat and sentenced Jesus to be scourged. After Jesus was scourged, the soldiers put a crown of thorn branches on his head, dressed him in a purple robe, shouted, "Hail, King of the Jews," and hit him with their fists. While Pilate was sitting on the judgment seat, two things happened: Pilate's wife sent him a message to not have anything to do with that innocent man, for she had had a very bad dream about him that day; and the chief priests and elders convinced the people to ask that Barabbas be set free and that Jesus be killed.

(69) After the scourging, Pilate went out to the people and said, "I'm going to have Jesus brought out to you so that you can see for yourselves that I think he's innocent." When Jesus came out wearing the crown of thorns and the purple robe, Pilate shouted, "Here he is!" When the chief priests and

officers saw Jesus, they cried out, "Crucify him, crucify him!" Pilate said, "You take him and crucify him yourselves because he's innocent." The Jews answered, "We have a law and by our law he ought to die because he made himself the Son of God." When Pilate heard this he was terrified and took Jesus back inside with him and asked, "Where do you come from?" When Jesus did not answer him, Pilate said, "How dare you not answer me! Don't you know I have the power to crucify you (70) or to set you free?" Jesus responded, "If God hadn't given you the power, you couldn't do anything to me! Therefore the ones who brought me to you have committed a worse sin." The internal strength exhibited by Jesus in this statement frightened Pilate terribly and from that point in time, Pilate tried to set Jesus free.

Pilate left the judgment hall and asked the multitude, "Which of these two men do you want me to release?" They said Barabbas. Pilate asked what he should do with Jesus. The Jews answered, "Crucify him." Pilate pleaded, "Why, what has he done wrong?" The Jews ignored Pilate's question and said, "Take this man away and crucify him, and release Barabbas." (71) Pilate wanted to release Jesus, so he asked again, "What should I do with Jesus?" The Jews said "Crucify him." Pilate asked again, "Why, what has he done wrong?" They cried out even louder, "Crucify him!" After Pilate asked what Jesus had done wrong the third time, he said, "I don't believe he has done anything worthy of death, so I will scourge him again and set him free." The people were in a frenzy and continued to scream for Jesus to be crucified and told Pilate, "If you let this man go, you are not Caesar's friend. Anyone who says he is a king is an enemy of Caesar." When Pilate heard this threat from the people, he knew he couldn't win, so he took water and washed his hands before the people, said he was innocent of the (72) murder of Jesus Christ, and showed the people his clean hands. The Jews responded, "His blood be on us and on our children."

Jesus was brought to the judgment seat where Pilate sentenced him to be crucified. Then Pilate released Barabbas. These things happened about 6 a.m.

Trying one last time to set Jesus free, Pilate brought Jesus to the people and said, "Look at your King!" The Jews cried out, "Take him away and crucify him." Pilate asked, "Do you want me to crucify your king?" The chief priests answered, "Caesar is our king." So after Pilate had Jesus scourged a second time, he ordered that he be crucified.

The Crucifixion

(74) After Jesus was scourged the second time, but before he was crucified, all the soldiers gathered in the armory where they stripped Jesus of his clothes, dressed him in a scarlet robe, put a crown of thorn branches on his head and put a stick in his right hand. They mocked him, bowing in front of him and saying, "Hail, King of the Jews!" (75) After they spit on him and hit him on the head with the stick, they dressed him in his own clothes and led him out to crucify him.

Jesus carried his own cross at first, but then a Cyrenian named Simon was forced to follow Jesus and carry the cross to Golgotha. As Jesus and the two criminals were led to Golgotha, Jesus told a group of women who were crying for him, "Don't cry for me, cry for yourselves and for your children. (76) For someday people will say, 'Women with no children are really lucky,' for at that time everyone will say to the mountains, 'Fall on us,' and to the hills 'Cover us.' For if they do these things in good times, what will they do when times are bad?"

At Golgotha, before Jesus was crucified, he refused a mixture of fluids that would have dulled the pain. Jesus and the two criminals were crucified during the same period of time; one of the criminals on Jesus' right side and the other on his left. During this period of time the following things also happened: Jesus asked his Father to forgive those who were crucifying him because they didn't really understand what they were doing; Pilate placed a placard on Jesus' cross which stated, "JESUS OF NAZARETH THE KING OF THE JEWS;" and (77) when the chief priests asked Pilate to change the wording on the placard, he wouldn't.

When the four soldiers finished crucifying Jesus, each soldier took some of Jesus' clothing. But since his coat was very valuable, they wouldn't tear it, so they cast lots for it. Jesus was crucified at 9 a.m. and as he hung on the cross (78) he was mocked by the soldiers, the people and the Jewish leaders.

Jesus Dies

(79) Some that passed by the cross said, "If you can destroy the temple and build it again in three days, save yourself. If you are the Son of God, come down from the cross." The chief priests told the scribes, "He saved others, but he can't save himself. If he's the King of Israel and can come down from the cross, we'll believe him. He trusted in God. Let God save him (80) if God wants to. This man even said he was the Son of God."

The thieves who were crucified with him also mocked him. Then one of the thieves said, "If you're the Messiah, save yourself and us." But the other thief said, "Don't you fear God? We're guilty! We deserve this! But this man didn't do anything wrong." Then he asked Jesus, "Lord, please remember me when you enter your kingdom." Jesus responded, "I tell you the truth, you will be with me in paradise."

Now from 12 noon to 3 p.m. the sky was dark. At 3 p.m. it got even darker and Jesus shouted, "My God, My God, Why have you left me?" (81) Some who stood near the cross said, "Listen to him, he's calling for Elijah."

Now Jesus' mother was standing by the cross with her sister and Mary, the wife of Cleophas, and Mary Magdalene. When Jesus saw his mother and John standing by, he said unto his mother, "Woman, this man is now your son." Then he said to John, "She is now your mother." From then on, John took care of Mary as if she were his own mother.

With his mother taken care of, Jesus knew he had finished everything he had to do. So he said, "I'm thirsty." One of the other Jews went to fill a sponge with fluid, but the others said, "Wait, let's see if Elijah will come to save him." (82) Since the other Jews wouldn't give Jesus anything to drink, his own disciples did. After Jesus drank the fluid and said, "It is finished," the top of the veil was torn in the middle. Then Jesus cried with a loud voice and said, "Father, my spirit is in your hands." After he cried aloud again, Jesus bowed his head and died. The tearing ended at the bottom of the veil, right after Jesus died.

Jesus' Burial

(83) When Jesus died the earth quaked, rocks were split apart, many of Jesus' disciples who had been dead were brought back to life and appeared to others in Jerusalem, and a centurion who stood at the cross said, "Truly, this man was the Son of God."

(84) Since the Jews didn't want the bodies to remain on the crosses on the annual sabbath day that would begin at sunset, they asked Pilate to break the legs of the three to hasten their deaths, and take their bodies down. The soldiers broke the legs of the two criminals. They didn't break Jesus' legs because he was already dead, but one of the soldiers did thrust a spear into Jesus' side, and blood and water came out. The crowd that had gathered to watch the crucifixion left. Jesus' disciples and the women who had followed Jesus from Galilee stood at a distance and watched as these things happened.

(85) As evening approached, Joseph of Arimathaea went boldly to Pilate and asked for Jesus' body to bury it. Pilate was surprised that Jesus was already dead (86) but gave the body to Joseph. Joseph had brought fine linen and Nicodemus had brought a mixture of spices, so they took the body of Jesus down, wrapped it in the linen with the spices, and placed it in a tomb. They rolled a huge stone to the door of the tomb, then left. (88) Mary Magdalene and Mary, the mother of Joses, had followed Joseph and Nicodemus to the tomb. After they saw where they laid Jesus' body, they returned to their homes.

The next day (the first day of unleavened bread), the chief priests and Pharisees went to Pilate and said, "While that liar was alive, he claimed that after he had been dead three days he would come back to life. So please set a guard at the tomb for three days to keep his disciples from stealing his body and saying that he has come back to life. If his disciples are able to do this, the last lie will be worse than the first one." Pilate agreed and (89) assigned soldiers to guard the tomb.

After the sabbath (the first day of unleavened bread) ended, Mary Magdalene, Mary the mother of James and Salome bought sweet spices and mixed them with ointments to anoint Jesus' body.

On the next day, the weekly sabbath, they rested.

Then on the first day of the week as it began to dawn, they came to the tomb to anoint Jesus' body with the spices they had prepared.

He Is Risen

As the women approached the tomb, (94) a great earthquake occurred as an angel descended from heaven, rolled back the stone from the door of the tomb, and sat on it. The angel's clothing was as white as snow and his appearance was so frightening that the soldiers guarding the tomb shook from fear and fainted. The women knew they weren't strong enough to roll the stone away from the door of the tomb, but found the stone rolled back when they arrived. The angel told the women, "Don't be afraid. I know you're looking for Jesus, but he's not here. He's risen. (95) Come and see where his body lay, then go and tell his disciples he's alive again and will meet them in Galilee."

The women didn't comprehend what the first angel said, so they entered the tomb still looking for Jesus' body. Instead they found another angel, who told them the same things the first angel did. The women still didn't comprehend that Jesus was alive, so two more angels appeared and asked them, "Why are you looking for the living in a place for the dead? Jesus isn't here! He's alive again. Don't you remember that he told you in Galilee (96) that he would be crucified, then rise from the dead the third day?" Then the women remembered what Jesus said and ran from the tomb to tell the disciples.

With the women on foot and the disciples in their own homes, it took time for the women to tell the disciples what they had seen. Initially the disciples didn't believe the women. But after Mary Magdalene told Peter and John, and they ran to the tomb (97) and looked inside, John believed. Peter and John returned to their homes, but Mary Magalene stood outside the tomb and wept.

When she looked into the tomb, she saw two angels sitting where Jesus' body had been. When the angels asked her why she was crying, she told them (98) that someone had removed Jesus' body and she didn't know where they had put it. Mary turned around and saw Jesus, but thought he was the gardener. When Jesus spoke to her, she recognized his voice and would have held him, but he said, "Don't hold on to me because I haven't seen my Father yet, but go and tell my disciples that I am going to my Father, and their Father; and to my God, and their God."

Mary went and told the disciples that she had see Jesus alive, and she told them what Jesus had said, but they didn't believe her. While Mary was doing this, Jesus went to heaven, returned to earth and appeared to the other women who were still telling the disciples what they had seen at the tomb. After these other women held Jesus by the feet and worshipped him, he told them to go and tell his (99) brethren to meet him in Galilee.

While the women went to tell the disciples, some of the soldiers who had been guarding the tomb came and told the chief priests what had happened. The priests bribed the soldiers and promised to protect them from the governor if they would just say that Jesus' disciples came during the night and took his body away while they were asleep. The soldiers took the money and did as they were told.

While the priests were bribing the soldiers, Jesus appeared in another form to two of his disciples as they walked to Emmaus, a village in the country. As the disciples were walking and talking about all the things that had happened, Jesus approached them and started walking with them. When Jesus asked them what they were discussing, one of the disciples said, "Are you the only person from Jerusalem who doesn't know what's happened there in the last few days?" Jesus asked, "What things?" They said,

"The things that happened to Jesus of Nazareth, a mighty prophet (100) who was crucified by the priests and rulers. And we had hoped that he would liberate Israel, but it has already been three days since all of this happened. Oh yes, some of the women with us surprised us when they told us that they were at the tomb this morning and didn't find Jesus' body, but saw angels who said Jesus was alive. Then some of the men went to the tomb and found it empty, but didn't see Jesus."

Then Jesus said, "You can be so foolish sometimes and so slow to believe what the prophets said. Christ was supposed to suffer these things and then be resurrected to glory!" Then Jesus began with the books in the Bible that Moses wrote and ended with the books that the prophets wrote, and explained everything written about himself in the scriptures.

(101) As they approached Emmaus, the two disciples invited Jesus to stay and eat with them. As they ate, Jesus blessed the bread and broke it. When Jesus gave the disciples the bread, they immediately recognized him and he vanished out of their sight.

On that same Sunday afternoon, the two disciples returned to Jerusalem and told the eleven apostles what had happened. The apostles did not believe them. Thomas was present when the two disciples told the apostles what they had seen, but Thomas left just before (102) Jesus appeared to the other apostles on this same Sunday afternoon.

Jesus' First Appearance to the Apostles After His Resurrection

The disciples were afraid of the Jewish leaders and had locked themselves in a room, when suddenly, Jesus was standing among them. After saying, "Peace be with you," Jesus showed them his hands and his side and the disciples were glad to see him. He told them they would be sent into the world to teach, as he had been sent. Then he breathed on them and said, "Receive the Holy Spirit."

Later when the other disciples told Thomas that they had seen Jesus, Thomas said, "Unless I see the print of the nails in his hands and put my finger into the (103) print

and put my hand into his side, I won't believe."

Jesus' Second Appearance to the Apostles

Eight days later, the apostles were together again and Thomas was present. With the doors locked again, Jesus suddenly appeared among them. The apostles were terrified because they thought Jesus was a ghost. Jesus asked them, "Why are you frightened? Why do you doubt? Its really me, fellows! Look at my hands and feet. Touch me and see. A ghost doesn't have flesh and bones like I do."

Then Jesus told Thomas, "Touch my hands and side, and don't doubt, but believe." Thomas (104) said, "My Lord and my God." Then Jesus said, "Thomas, because you have seen me, you've believed, but those people who will believe in me without seeing me will really be blessed."

While the disciples sat in utter amazement, Jesus asked, "Do you have anything to eat?" They gave him a piece of fish and a honeycomb. After he ate, he did other things to show his disciples he was really alive.

Then Jesus told them, "When I was with you before I died, I told you that everything written about me by Moses and the prophets and in the psalms had to happen." After this, he helped them understand the scriptures and said, "The scriptures say (105) that it was necessary for Christ to suffer all the things he suffered and then to rise from the dead the third day. They also say that repentance and forgiveness of sins must be preached in my name among all nations, beginning at Jerusalem. So I want you to go into the world and preach the good news to everyone. Anyone who believes and is baptized will be saved. Anyone who doesn't believe will be condemned and I will perform these signs for those who believe: they will cast out demons in my name, they will speak in different languages, and if they pick up serpents or drink any deadly thing they won't be hurt. They will also place their hands on the sick, and the sick will be healed."

"Remember! I will send you the promise of my Father, but wait in Jerusalem until you receive God's Holy Spirit."

Then Jesus led the disciples out to Bethany and raised his hands and blessed them. (106) As he was blessing them he was taken away to heaven. After the disciples worshipped him, they returned to Jerusalem joyfully and stayed primarily in the temple, praising and blessing God.

Jesus' Third Appearance to the Apostles

Some time after the day of Pentecost, the eleven apostles left Jerusalem and went to Galilee where Jesus appeared to them for the third time. Peter, Thomas, Nathaniel, James, John and two other disciples were together at the sea of Galilee when Peter said he was going fishing. The others went along and they fished all night, but caught nothing. When morning came, the disciples didn't recognize Jesus as he stood on the shore and (107) asked them what they had caught. They said nothing, so he told them to cast their net on the right side of the boat. When they did, they caught so many fish that they couldn't pull the net into the boat. When John told Peter it was Jesus on the shore, Peter wrapped his clothes around him, dove into the water and swam to shore. The other disciples followed in the boat, pulling the net.

As soon as they reached the shore, they saw fish being cooked on a fire and bread. When Jesus asked for some of the fish they caught, Peter pulled the net to shore and even though the net was filled with one hundred and fifty-three large fish, (108) it didn't tear. Jesus invited the disciples to eat breakfast and served them the bread and fish. When they finished eating, Jesus asked Peter if he loved him more than the other disciples did. Peter answered, "Yes, Lord, you know I love you." Jesus told him, "Feed my lambs." When Jesus asked Peter again if he loved him, Peter answered, "Yes, Lord, you know that I love you." Jesus said, "Feed my sheep." When Jesus asked Peter if he loved him a third time, Peter was upset and said, "Lord, you know everything, and you (109) know that I love you." After Jesus told Peter, "Feed my sheep," he described how Peter would die and honor God. After Jesus told Peter to follow him, Peter turned, saw John following, and asked Jesus, "What will he do?" Jesus answered, "If I want him to live until I return, what is that to you? Follow me." Because of this, a rumor spread among the disciples that John wouldn't die. But that isn't what Jesus said at all! He said, "If I want him to live until I return what is that to you?"

Jesus' Fourth Appearance to the Apostles

(110) Later, the eleven original apostles went to a mountain in Galilee where Jesus had told them to meet. When they saw him, they worshipped him, but some still doubted that it was Jesus. Jesus approached them and said, "I have been given all power in heaven and earth so I want you to go into all nations and teach. People will come to you and want to become my disciples. Baptize these people into the name of the Father, and of the Son, and of the Holy Spirit, and teach them to do everything I have commanded you. And remember, I will always be with you, even to the end of this age. After this, Jesus returned to heaven and sat at the right side of God. (111) The apostles went and preached everywhere and the miracles Jesus performed proved that he fully supported them. Amen.

GLOSSARY

The explanation of the terms in this glossary comes from three sources: the American Heritage Dictionary (abbreviated AHD), Halley's Bible Handbook (HBH) and Strong's Exhaustive Concordance of the Bible, Greek Dictionary (the SEC abbreviation is accompanied by the reference number in the Greek Dictionary).

Abba: Father (SEC #5).

abide: to stay in a given place, dwell, tarry, remain (SEC #3306).

affirm: to declare positively; maintain to be true (AHD).

agony: the suffering of intense physical and mental pain, anguish (AHD, SEC #74).

anguish: an agonizing physical or mental pain; torment, torture (AHD).

anodyne: a medicine able to soothe or relieve pain (AHD).

anoint: to oil with perfume; to put oil on (AHD, SEC #218).

apostle: a messenger who is sent to teach (SEC #652).

behoved: to be necessary, must, need, ought, should (SEC #1163).

bewray: to disclose, especially inadvertently, betray (AHD, SEC #1212).

besought: past tense of beseech, to urgently request, implore; earnest request (AHD).

betray: to give information to an enemy; to commit treason against or be a traitor (AHD).

blasphemy: any contemptuous or profane act, utterance, or writing concerning God (AHD).

Calvary: a hill outside the ancient city of Jerusalem where Jesus was crucified (AHD).

chief priest: a high ranking priest (SEC #749).

comforter: one who comforts; the Holy Spirit; an intercessor, consoler (AHD, SEC #3875).

concordance: an alphabetical index of all words in a text (AHD).

constrain: confine; compel; restrain; force; unnatural (AHD, SEC #315).

contradiction: discrepancy; something that contains contradictory elements (AHD).

convocation: a group of people assembled by summons, called together (AHD, SEC #4744).

counsel: exchange opinions or ideas; advice or guidance (AHD).

cross: a cross, stake or post (set upright) used as an instrument of capital punishment (SEC #4716).

crucifixion: Roman punishment for slaves, foreigners, and criminals who were not Roman citizens; the most agonizing and ignominious death a cruel age could devise. Nails were driven through the hands and feet, and the victim was left hanging there in agony, starvation, insufferable thirst and excruciating convulsions of pain. Death usually followed in four to six days. In Jesus' case it was over in six hours (HBH).

crucify: to put to death by crucifixion (AHD).

damsel: a young woman or girl; maiden (AHD).

defile: to make filthy or dirty, to render impure, corrupt; to profane or sully (a good name or reputation, for example; to make unclean or unfit for ceremonial use; desecrate AHD).

disciple: a pupil, learner, person who subscribes to the teachings of a master and assists in spreading them (AHD, SEC #3101).

earnest: determined, eager, showing deep sincerity or feeling, serious (AHD).

elder: an older; a senior (also figuratively, member of the celestial council) (SEC #4245).

exceedingly: more abundant (SEC #4056).

exhaustive: comprehensive; thorough (AHD).

expedient: appropriate to the purpose at hand; serving to promote one's interest (AHD).

forthwith: at once; immediate; right away (AHD).

furlong: a unit for measuring distance, equal to 1/8 mile or 220 yards (AHD).

gall: poison or an anodyne (wormwood, poppy, etc.) (AHD, SEC #5521).

Gethsemane: a garden near the foot of the western slope of the Mount of Olives (HBH).

gird: to bind, especially with a belt (SEC #2224).

Golgotha: the skull (from the shape of the hill), a knoll near Jerusalem, the hill of Calvary where Jesus was crucified (AHD, SEC #1115).

goodman: the head of the family; master of the house; a male head of a household; a householder, homeowner (AHD, SEC #3617).

gospel: good news, good tidings (Strong's #2097).

guestchamber: a room in a house, especially a bedroom for guests, a suite of rooms, a hall for the meeting of an assembly, a lodging-place, inn (AHD and SEC #2646).

hewn: quarried or cut in stone (SEC #2991).

hitherto: until this time; up till now (AHD).

hyssop: a woody plant, native to Asia having spikes of small blue flowers and aromatic leaves used in perfumery and as a condiment. It is also used as the source of twigs used for sprinkling in certain purificatory rites (AHD).

insurrection: an act of open revolt or rebellion

against civil authority (AHD).

interrelate: to place in mutual relationship (AHD).

Iscariot: the inhabitant of the area of Kerioth (SEC #2469).

lament: to bewail, mourn (SEC #2354).

lot: a die (for drawing chances) (SEC #2819, 2806).

manifest: to show, reveal, make plain or apparent to the sight or understanding (AHD).

Messias: Messiah (Christ) (AHD, SEC #3323).

mingle: to mix or combine (AHD).

myrrh: a sweet smelling plant or bush used as a narcotic (SEC #4669).

narrative: a story or description of actual or fictional events, narrated account (AHD).

overcome: to defeat in competition or conflict, conquer, overpower, be victorious (AHD).

paraphrase: a restatement of a text or passage in other words, often to clarify meaning (AHD).

Passover: an offering. Animal sacrifice or offering in Old Testament; human sacrifice or offering in New Testament which was Jesus Christ. The festival of sacrifices. On the 14th day of the first month, Nisan, this day is kept to commemorate the sparing of the lives of the children of Israel when the death angel passed over, and then Christ being crucified and becoming our Passover Lamb for the forgiveness of our sins (AHD, SEC #6453, 3957).

Passover lamb: a member of a flock, a lamb, a male without spot or blemish, within the first year; Christ our Passover Lamb (SEC #7716, 2089, 3957, 6453).

Pharisee: a separatist, exclusively religious; a member of an ancient Jewish sect that emphasized strict interpretation and observance of the Mosaic law in both its oral and written form (AHD, SEC #5330).

Pontius Pilate: the Roman governor of Judea (26-37 A.D.). He assumed office about the time that Jesus began his public ministry. He was merciless, cruel and noted for his habitual brutality (HBH).

potter's field: a place for the burial of indigent or unknown persons (AHD).

precede: to come before in time, order or rank; exist or occur prior to (AHD).

prevail: to be greater in strength or influence, to triumph or win a victory (AHD).

prophecy: a prediction or revelation transmitted orally or in writing (AHD).

purge: to clean perfectly (SEC #1245).

rebuke: to criticize or reprove sharply; reprimand; admonish (AHD, SEC #2008).

redeem: to recover ownership by paying a specified sum; to pay off; to fulfill an oath, pledge, or promise; to rescue or ransom; save from a state of sinfulness and its consequences; to make up for (AHD, SEC #3085).

reference: the act of referring to; the state of being related or referred (AHD).

sabbath: the seventh day of the week, Saturday, named in the Ten Commandments as the day of rest and worship (AHD, SEC #4521).

sanctify: to make pure, blameless, Holy, most Holy (SEC #37, 40).

scourge: to whip; usually preceded capital punishment. Scourging was done with a whip which was made of a number of leather thongs weighted with pieces of lead or sharp metal. The victim was stripped to the waist, then bound, in a bent-over position, to a post, and beaten on the bare back with the scourge till the flesh was torn open. Sometimes death resulted (HBH).

scribe: public clerk or secretary; professional copyist of manuscripts or documents (AHD, SEC #1122).

sedition: an uprising, controversy; dissension, insurrection, conduct or language inciting to rebellion against the authority of the state; a going apart (AHD, SEC #4714, 2476).

sepulchre: a burial place, tomb, grave; a tomb cut into a wall of solid rock with a trench in front where the stone rolled to the door (SEC #3419, HBH).

sequence: the following of one thing after another, succession; an order of succession; arrangement; related to or continuous series (AHD).

servile: work of any kind, labor, bondage, service (SEC #5656).

smite: to slap with the palm of the hand; to "thump", pummel with a stick, but in any case by repeated blows (SEC #4474, 5180, 3960).

sop: to dip, soak thoroughly in a liquid; a bit of bread or other food soaked in a liquid (AHD).

stave: a stick or club (SEC #3586).

straightway: instantly, immediately, soon, presently (SEC #3916, 2117).

synagogue: specifically Jewish, a meeting or place; by analogy, a Christian church; assembly, (SEC #4864).

tarry: to delay or be late in going or coming; linger; to wait; to remain or stay temporarily, as in a place; sojourn (AHD).

temptation: the act of tempting or the condition of being enticed; alluring, seductive (AHD).

threescore: sixty (SEC #1835, 1803).

thrice: three times (AHD).

tomb: a grave, place of burial, sepulchre; a vault or chamber serving as a repository for the dead (AHD, SEC #3419).

transgressor: without law, lawless, unlawful, wicked (SEC #459).

translate: to express in another language, to put in simpler terms (AHD).

travail: strenuous mental or physical exertion; labor; toil; tribulation or agony; anguish; the labor of childbirth (AHD, SEC #3205, 5088).

tumult: the din or commotion of a great crowd; a disorderly commotion or disturbance; a tempestuous act, as an uprising; agitation of the mind or emotions (AHD).

unleavened: made without leavening or rising agent (yeast) (AHD, SEC #4682).

vehemently: characterized by forcefulness of expression or intensity of emotion, passion, or conviction, ardent, emphatic; marked by or full of vigor or energy; strong; violent; excessive, (AHD, SEC #4053, 1171, 2159).

wont: being accustomed to, likely, to be in the habit of (AHD).

LIST OF CHARACTERS

The information on this list of characters comes from three sources: the American Heritage Dictionary, Halley's Bible Handbook and Strong's Exhaustive Concordance of the Bible, Greek Dictionary.

apostles: Simon: name was changed to Peter by Jesus; in the fishing business with James and John; energetic, enthusiastic, impulsive, impetuous, a natural born leader; generally the spokesman for the twelve. Andrew: Peter's brother; one of first converts with John. James and John: sons of Zebedee. Philip: a fellow-townsman of Peter and Andrew who brought Bartholomew whose surname was Nathaniel. Thomas: a twin; cautious, thoughtful, skeptical, gloomy. Matthew: a publican. James: the son of Alphaeus, called "The Little", probably because of his stature. Lebbaeus: his surname was Thaddaeus. Simon: the Zealot and a Canaanite (the Zealots were an intensely nationalistic sect, directly opposite to the publicans). Judas Iscariot: the betrayer of Jesus for thirty pieces of silver, of Kerioth, a town of Judah; the only non-Galilean apostle; avaricious, dishonest, expected rich reward when his Master was seated on the throne of David; disappointed when he saw his worldly dream fade; after his hideous crime, hanged himself.

Annas: father-in-law to the high priest, Caiaphas; had tremendous influence with the high priest; his family had become wealthy through the trading booths in the Temple.

Barabbas: murderer and robber who was released instead of Jesus.

Caesar: title of the Roman Emperor.

Caiaphas: high priest of the Hebrew nation; was primarily responsible for Jesus' crucifixion.

Comforter: see Holy Ghost.

Cyrenian: see Simon.

damsel: young female slave, servant, bondmaid.

Elias: Elijah, Hebrew prophet of the ninth century B.C.

goodman: head of a family, householder, master of the house.

Governor: see Pontius Pilate.

Herod: the ruler over Galilee at the time of Jesus' trial, also responsible for the death of John the Baptist.

Holy Ghost: Holy Spirit, Spirit of God, Spirit of truth, Comforter.

Jesus: The Word, Christ, Son of God, Son of Man. He was born as a human to be the sacrificial Lamb of God for the forgiveness of our sins.

Jeremy: Jeremiah, a prophet in the old Testament.

Joanna: one of the women who went with Mary Magdalene to anoint Jesus' body; wife of Herod's steward from the palace.

Joseph: a man from Arimathea, an honourable counsellor, who along with Nicodemus, asked for Jesus' body for burial.

Mary: mother of Jesus Christ.

Mary: wife of Cleophas; Mary's sister (also at the crucifixion).

Mary: mother of James the less, Joses, and Salome; mother of Zebedee's children (went to the tomb with Mary Magdalene).

Mary Magdalene: the first person to whom Jesus appeared after his resurrection; healed of seven demons by Jesus.

Nicodemus: went with Joseph to ask for the body of Jesus.

Pontius Pilate: Roman governor of Judea (26-37 A.D.); assumed office about the time Jesus began his public ministry; official residence at Caesarea; came to Jerusalem at the time of the Jewish feasts to keep order; merciless, cruel, noted for his habitual brutality; enjoyed the spectacle of torture and death (he mingled the blood of Galileans with their sacrifices, Luke 13:1). Jesus made a tremendous impression on this hard-hearted Roman governor. Pilate wanted to escape responsibility for Jesus' death and tried desperately to release Jesus. He had Jesus scourged in the hope that the Jews would be satisfied with partial punishment, and not require that Jesus be crucified. He did not decide to crucify Jesus until it looked as if he might lose his position as Governor of Judea. Pilate is said to have committed suicide. Pilate's wife, Procula, is said to have become a Christian.

satan: the god of this world (II Corinthians 4:4), the prince of the power of the air (Ephesians 2:2), the deceiver of the whole world (Revelation 12:9, 20:3, 8, 10), the great dragon and the old serpent (Revelation 12:9;20:2), the prince of this world (John 16:11).

Simon: a Cyrenian who was compelled to carry Jesus' cross.

Son of Man: a name for Jesus.

BIBLIOGRAPHY

The Holy Bible, King James Version, Reference Red Letter edition, World Bible Publishers, Iowa Falls, Iowa 50126

The Holy Bible New King James Version, Copyright 1982 Thomas Nelson, Inc., Thomas Nelson Publishers, Nashville - Camden - New York

The Holy Bible, New International Version, Copyright 1982, by Zondervan Corporation, Zondervan Bible Publishers, Grand Rapids, Michigan

The Holy Bible, Revised Standard Version, New Testament Copyright 1946, Old Testament, Copyright 1952, American Bible Society, New York

The Holy Bible, Comtemporary English Version, God's Promise for People of Today, Thomas Nelson Publishers, Nashville, Atlanta, London, Vancouver

The Living Bible, Paraphrased, A Thought-for-Thought Translation, Copyright 1971 by Tyndale House Publishers, Inc., Wheaton, Illinois 60189

The New Scofield Reference Bible, King James Version Copyright 1967, Oxford University Press, Inc., New York

Twenty-six Translations of The Bible, Volume III, New Testament, Copyright 1967, 1973, 1985, The Zondervan Corporation, Grand Rapids, Michigan, Distributed by American Home Libraries, Inc., Published by Mathis Publishers, Inc., Atlanta, Georgia 30341

Halley's Bible Handbook, An Abbreviated Bible Commentary, by Henry H. Halley, Twenty-Fourth Edition, Copyright 1965, Zondervan Publishing House, Grand Rapids, Michigan

Strong's Exhaustive Concordance of the Bible, by James Strong, S.T.D., LL.D., together with Dictionaries of the Original Hebrew Old Testament and the Greek New Testament, Holman Bible Publishers, Nashville, Tennessee

The American Heritage Dictionary of the English Language, New College Edition, Published by Houghton Mifflin Company, Boston, Massachusetts

INDEX

134

G

gall, 76
Galilaean, 57, 59, 66
garden, 4, 6, 8, 11, 41-43, 54, 57, 59, 86, 119, 120, 122
gardener, 98, 117, 126
Gethsemane, 2, 7-9, 11, 27, 35, 36, 38, 112, 119
Golgotha, 5, 74, 76, 124
goodman, 4, 8, 11, 13, 21, 26, 27, 35, 56, 87, 112
governor, 1, 4, 5, 62, 64, 65, 67, 70, 74, 99, 126, 130
grave, 83, 89, 90
guilty, 50, 118, 122, 123, 125
guestchamber, 13

H

hall, 4, 46, 47, 53, 62-64, 69, 70, 74, 124
hands, 1, 7, 8, 15, 16, 41, 42, 44, 45, 49, 50, 68, 71, 81, 82, 90, 96, 102, 105, 109, 115, 121, 124, 125, 127-129
hanged, 62, 80,122
Herod, 66-68, 123
Holy Ghost, 24, 106, 110, 116-118, 127, 128
hour, 2, 3, 7, 8, 9, 11, 13, 33, 35, 36, 37, 38, 41, 42, 45, 54, 58, 72, 73, 77, 78, 80, 81, 93, 101, 112, 119, 122
house, 4, 8, 11-13, 21, 26, 27, 35, 46, 56, 87, 112, 114, 116, 117, 121
hyssop, 82

I

innocent, 1, 62, 72, 122-124

J

James, 7, 9, 11, 36, 84, 89, 92, 96, 119, 126, 128
Jesus of Nazareth, 43, 50, 51, 52, 58, 76, 95, 99, 120, 124, 127
Joseph, 6, 83, 85, 86, 125
Judas, 3, 4, 8, 14, 15, 18, 24, 41-44, 62, 101, 114-117, 120-122
judgment, 4, 31, 32, 62-64, 68-70, 72, 118, 123, 124

K

kiss, 8, 43, 44, 121
King, 1, 5, 63-64, 68-70, 71, 72, 74, 76-80, 116, 123-125
kingdom, 6, 13-15, 20, 64, 79, 80, 85, 114-116, 123-125
kneeled, 8, 9, 10, 11, 37, 119

L

lamb, 12, 87, 108, 114

legs, 83, 84, 125
lots, 5, 77, 125

M

maid, 50-55, 57, 58, 122
manifested, 39
Mary Magdalene, 6, 81, 84, 88, 89, 91-93, 96, 98, 125, 126
Master, 13, 14, 16, 44, 90, 98, 114, 121
mocked, 50, 61, 66, 74, 75, 78, 79, 122, 124, 125
morning, 6, 61, 87-90, 93, 106, 112, 124-128
mount of Olives, 3, 8, 26, 27, 117
multitude, 1, 3, 4, 8, 42, 45, 62, 67, 68, 70, 71, 107, 113, 124
myrrh, 76, 86

N

new testament, 10, 15

P

palace, 42, 46, 47, 50, 52
parted, 5, 62, 77, 106
pass, 7-10, 17, 25, 30, 36, 37, 75, 79, 95, 97, 99, 101, 106, 125
passover, 2, 4, 11, 12, 13, 62, 67, 68, 72, 86-89, 112, 114, 115, 122, 123
Pavement, 72
peace, 24, 36, 49, 102, 103, 113, 117, 119, 127
Peter, 2, 4, 7, 9, 11, 12, 16, 18, 20, 21, 35, 36, 42, 44-47, 50-61, 87, 95-97, 106-109, 112, 114-116, 119, 121, 122, 126, 128
Pharisees, 3, 4, 42, 88-91, 126
Philip, 22, 116
pierced, 84, 85
Pilate, 1, 2, 4-6, 62-72, 76, 84-86, 88-92, 112, 122-126
potter's field, 63
Praetorium, 74
preparation, 12, 72, 84-88, 91
pray, 7-11, 20, 23, 34, 36-40, 45, 119, 120
prayer, 7-11, 37, 38, 41, 112, 119, 120
prepare, 2, 11-13, 21, 88-90, 92, 93, 114, 116, 126
prophet, 45, 63, 77, 90, 99, 100, 104, 127

R

reed, 48, 74, 75, 81
release, 67-72, 112, 123, 124
remembrance, 15, 24
resurrection, 2, 3, 83, 90, 102, 112, 113, 127
repentance, 105, 127
rise, 8, 10, 11, 15, 38, 41, 42, 88, 90, 91, 96, 97, 105, 119, 126, 127
risen, 35, 56, 88, 92-95, 98, 101, 103, 108, 112, 126
robe, 66, 68, 70, 74, 75, 123, 124

135